JUBILEE

A SEASON OF SPIRITUAL RENEWAL

MEL LAWRENZ

Regal

From Gospel Light
Ventura, California, U.S.A.

Published by Regal
From Gospel Light
Ventura, California, U.S.A.
www.regalbooks.com
Printed in the U.S.A.

Library of Congress Cataloging-in-Publication Data
Lawrenz, Mel.
Jubilee : a season of spiritual renewal / Mel Lawrenz.
p. cm.
ISBN 978-0-8307-4636-1 (trade paper)
1. Rest—Religious aspects—Christianity. 2. Spiritual healing.
3. Spiritual life. I. Title.
BV4597.55.L39 2008
269'.6—dc22
2008019405

1 2 3 4 5 6 7 8 9 10 / 15 14 13 12 11 10 09 08

FOR CHRISTOPHER—
EVERYTHING *IS* DIFFERENT.

CONTENTS

PREFACE

It is an astonishing thing to watch thousands of people experience a season of spiritual renewal together. I had the special blessing of watching that happen at Elmbrook Church over a year-long season we called "Jubilee," which focused on the extraordinary Year of Jubilee described in the Old Testament, a season to renew the core of spiritual life.

Anyone can enter a period of Jubilee at any time, and in this book you'll be led through a seven-week season of spiritual renewal. Each week corresponds to one of the seven themes of Jubilee: Sabbath, redemption, freedom, forgiveness, healing, justice and proclamation, each one a life-changing truth. Some of them may be familiar to you, others not. What we discovered is that plunging into a theme like Sabbath (learning God's rhythm of work and rest, and letting go of control so that we can know that God and God alone is in control) was life-giving and life-changing for all of us. And we also discovered that while we may have thought we understood a truth like forgiveness, it is possible to live for years not knowing the depths of what true forgiveness means.

This book is for you, friend, as a way to begin a journey of spiritual renewal. As you prepare to set out, be assured of this: If you grasp more fully just one of these seven Jubilee truths, and if it becomes real in your life, you will be changed forever.

—Mel Lawrenz

HOW TO USE THIS BOOK

The 50-day spiritual growth season you are about to experience is an opportunity for you to explore seven important spiritual truths and let them transform your life:

Week 1—*Sabbath*: rehearsing that God and God alone is in control

Week 2—*Redemption*: being freed by God's great acts of deliverance

Week 3—*Freedom*: cherishing the liberty that God brings to every area of life

Week 4—*Forgiveness*: accepting the mercy of God and letting go of those you've held in debt

Week 5—*Healing*: letting God restore your spirit, your body and your relationships

Week 6—*Justice*: standing for what is right and being an advocate for the downtrodden

Week 7—*Proclamation*: knowing what you stand for and letting others know it

Each week's theme begins with a short chapter that explores how that theme is tied to Jubilee. The chapter is followed by seven "Daily Reflections." You can either read the chapter at the beginning of the week and then focus on the devotions for the remaining days, or you can read one or two sections of the chapter each day, alongside the Daily Reflections.

You will get the most out of this 50-day Jubilee experience if you:

1. Read each day's Scripture passage carefully. Open your Bible and read the context of the passage. Use a translation of the Bible you are comfortable with. A "study Bible" edition will have helpful notes, and you may even want to use a Bible dictionary or commentary for reference to deepen your understanding.

2. Read the Daily Reflection (and take a few minutes to reflect!).

3. Find some time during the day to do the application activity suggested by the "Make It Real" section.

4. Talk to God about what you are learning. Each day, thank Him for something new you have learned. When the "Make It Real" section suggests you pray about an issue, take the opportunity to pray. God's truths are anchored in our hearts when we talk to Him about them. Write in the margins of this book or use your own journal to record your thoughts.

You can enter a Jubilee season of spiritual renewal on your own, with your family, with a small group or with an entire church. Here's how:

1. Pick a time to read the introduction, "Preparing for Jubilee." This will set the stage for you. Next, decide

whether you will go through Jubilee on your own or with someone else, and then choose a seven-week period (50 days) during which you will cover the seven themes.

2. Plan for 20 to 30 minutes per day to give yourself time to reflect and meditate on the ideas.

3. If you are going through the seven weeks of Jubilee with someone else (your family, a small group), meet weekly to talk about what you are learning. Use the discussion questions at the end of each week's section. You can also find helpful supplemental materials at www.elmbrookjubilee.org.

4. Plan some kind of celebration at the end of the seven weeks, whether on your own or with the people who have joined you for Jubilee.

5. Commit to prayer, asking God to continue to make Sabbath, redemption, freedom, forgiveness, healing, justice and proclamation real in your life.

PREPARING FOR JUBILEE

Sometimes a public announcement changes life forever.

Consider a major press conference at Johns Hopkins or a similarly prestigious medical school. At a table, five medical researchers are seated, and one rises to the microphone to say: "Ladies and gentlemen, we are here today to announce that we believe we will soon be able to reverse any and all forms of human cancer. *We have found a cure for cancer.*" I wonder if a day like that will ever come—I certainly hope so. I can only imagine all the lives that would be changed. Right now I only know the reality that cancer causes suffering and death.

Or consider June 6, 1944. Europeans listened to their radios as the calm steady voice of Dwight D. Eisenhower, Supreme Commander of the Allied Forces in World War II, spoke these words: "People of Western Europe: A landing was made this morning on the coast of France by troops of the Allied Expeditionary Force. . . . the hour of your liberation is approaching."[1] This was the word they had been waiting for, the word they couldn't help but hope for—though no one, before the landing at Normandy, could have guaranteed that a breach of the entrenched Nazi enemy was possible. D-Day could have been "defeat day," but the words of General Eisenhower told a different story.

While I don't know if we will ever develop a cure for cancer, I do know the world was liberated from tyranny in World War II (although as long as tyranny is an impulse in the human heart, wars in the world will go on). I also know that as life-changing as Eisenhower's words were, they pale in comparison to the most hope-filled announcement I have ever heard: the words spoken by Jesus nearly 2,000 years ago at the start of His public life in a small synagogue in a no-name, backwater town. No other public speech has given me as much encouragement, confidence and patience as His words.

Jesus' first recorded public speech is brief, pointed and outrageously confident. It is about cures and liberation and justice. It is a word about the inception of a new reign—smaller, at that point, than a mustard seed. And if it is true, if any part of it is true, nothing will ever be the same again. Yet to fully appreciate the impact of that word, we must hear it uttered from His lips, in the synagogue at Nazareth, in "the acceptable year of the Lord"—that is, in "Jubilee."

The synagogue at Nazareth would have been a modest structure built of stones and timbers, with a stone-tile floor and a few windows large enough to let in fresh air and light, but not so large as to compromise the privacy of the place. It was likely one room, furnished with simple benches around the perimeter to make the empty space in the middle where readings and teachings occurred the center of focus. The Jewish synagogue (which means literally "bringing together") was an invention of necessity during those terrible centuries when the Temple of Jerusalem, built by Solomon, lay in ruins, and the Jews were scattered by a long succession of tyrants throughout the whole

Mediterranean world, from Palestine to Rome to North Africa. These meeting places were small, decentralized congregations that preserved the Torah and the worship of God. (Eventually the early Christian church took the same form of distributed congregations, meeting in homes, and then in designated buildings.) Synagogues were all about the assembly of people, not the building. And so a small group would have gathered regularly in the synagogue of Nazareth, reminding themselves and others that even out there in the north, in "Galilee of the Gentiles," the God of Abraham, Isaac and Jacob was still remembered and obeyed.

Nazareth was Jesus' hometown. He had just returned, having spent 40 days and 40 nights fasting in the desert, enduring temptation and emerging victorious. Following that, Jesus began circulating among the synagogues of Galilee, teaching something new. We learn exactly what He was teaching when He came to His hometown and went to the synagogue on a Sabbath day.

Jesus knew the men who had gathered in the room, and they knew Him. The progression of prayers and songs went on as they usually did. The presiding elder handed a Scripture scroll to the son of Joseph of Nazareth. The scroll made a shuffling noise as Jesus unrolled it, looking for the specific passage in Isaiah's book of prophecy that He wanted to read (we know it as chapter 61, though they didn't have chapters as such in those days). Someone in the corner might have caught himself yawning. Another, gazing out the small window. Someone else, thinking about his donkey that had stumbled and broken his leg the day before.

It was just another day at the synagogue.

Then life changed suddenly—and forever—as Jesus made His public announcement:

> The Spirit of the Lord is on me, because he has anointed me to preach good news to the poor. He has sent me to proclaim freedom for the prisoners and recovery of sight for the blind, to release the oppressed, to proclaim the year of the Lord's favor (Luke 4:18-19).

He rolled up the scroll, handed it to the attendant and sat down. For some reason that we can only guess, in the reading of these few words Jesus captivated the attention of everyone in the synagogue. Luke, who relates the details of the account, says that "the eyes of everyone were fastened on him" (v. 20). It wasn't that the words were new to the listeners—this part of Isaiah's prophesy was thoroughly known and cherished by the Jews, as it was a solemn promise of Yahweh to His beloved people. Something that sustained their hope. The people had been waiting for generations to see a new era of liberty. To see something *really* happen.

And then came an astonishing statement from Jesus, His eyes scanning His small audience: "Today, this Scripture is fulfilled in your hearing" (v. 21).

Scripture—the "sacred writing," a word that evokes confidence, because it's rooted in the character of the Creator Himself and etched in history.

Fulfilled—an alarming word that claims, "*This*—which you see happening now—is *that*—which you heard the prophets predict."

Today—this word is the lynchpin. "*Today*, this Scripture is fulfilled in your hearing." We don't know whether this is all Jesus said, or if He went on to comment further, but we do know the result: "All spoke well of him and were amazed at the gracious words that came from his lips. 'Isn't this Joseph's son?' they asked" (v. 22).

It is not likely that anyone in the room fully believed in that moment that God's kingdom had come with the coming of Jesus—just as today nobody would take seriously a medical intern at a hospital running through the halls announcing that he was about to deliver the cure for cancer. But the people liked what they heard. There was a graciousness in what Jesus said, perhaps a ring of truth. Everyone knew that there were covert political movements in place to try to oust the Romans from Israel. Maybe this was the time—somehow, somewhere.

But the mood in the room plummeted with Jesus' next words: "I tell you the truth, no prophet is accepted in his hometown" (v. 24). They had to wonder: *Was He calling Himself a prophet? Was He predicting that the people of Nazareth would reject the movement of God, no matter where it came from?* And then it got worse. Jesus reminded them that the great prophets Elijah and Elisha were sometimes sent to people outside Israel to perform signs and miracles. The message stung: *Today* is the time; but *you* will not see it, understand it or accept it.

And now, when His words became confrontational, the same people who had been spellbound and enamored with Jesus' gracious words became livid. Rationality gave way to fury. The group physically moved against Jesus. They shoved and pushed Jesus out the door. They kept going. They drove him further. They went right to the edge of town–which happened to be a cliff.

"Shove Him away!"

"Get rid of this deranged man who holds out a promise in one hand and slaps us in the face with the other!"

And Jesus would have gone over the cliff, but somehow, miraculously, He "walked right through the crowd and went on his way" (v. 30).

That was quite a day, the day that God's war on evil and injustice and disease was publicly announced. On that day, everything changed.

I have met all kinds of people who are consumed with one desire: *Something has to change. Something has to be different in my life. I don't want to go on this way. I don't see how I can go on like this.*

Now, there are times when we think, *Something has to be different*, though we shouldn't because the motive is envy ("I hope my brother goes bankrupt") or greed ("I can't be happy until I'm a millionaire") or lust ("I know she's married, but I must have her") or a dozen other rotten impulses.

But I find that most people who want things to be different have understandable, legitimate reasons.

"I want the doctor to give me some other diagnosis than MS."

"I've got to get out of this credit card hole I've dug myself into."

"Something has got to change in my marriage before it all falls apart."

"My kid has to get his feet on the ground."

"I've got to convince the parole board."

"Someone has to help me break this addiction."

"The judge has to listen to my side of the case."

"I've got to get some rest."

"I need to find a purpose for my life."

"I need to figure out a way to forgive my father."

On and on. Our aspirations and our desperation keep rising up from some deep place inside. Or is it that they come to us from the outside—like God prodding us along, not letting us settle for mediocrity? Not wanting us to lose hope. Telling us this mystery: That we have to accept life the way it is, but we should at the same time long for everything to be different.

Does that sound like a flat-out contradiction?

It isn't a contradiction, but a paradox. The Bible teaches plainly that nothing is perfect in this life, although everything could have been perfect and will one day be made perfect as it was meant to be. So what do we do now? Accept things the way they are, or hope for and strive for something better? Do we say, "The way things are must be God's will, so I had better not fight against it"? Or do we say, "God's will is that things should change for the better. Redemption of life has already begun, even though we will realize its fullness only in the next life"? All the truths of Jubilee lead us in the second direction. With the coming of Jesus, everything has begun to change.

So we accept the reality that we are all sinners and we are going to sin—but we don't acquiesce to the inevitability. We accept disease and accidental injury, but we still pray for healing (and rightly so) and try to drive our cars responsibly. We accept the forgiveness of Jesus, but we also admit that we will have to be forgivers of others for the rest of our lives.

The public announcement Jesus made in the synagogue of Nazareth was essentially this: Everything is different now in that a power has come into the world, the power of the kingdom of God. God "has anointed me" means "I have been sent. I am the Chosen One. I am on a mission. I'm about to get to work." It also means "I am Messiah." (In Hebrew: *Messiach*. In Greek: *Christos*. In English: Christ.)

Jesus announced "good news to the poor," "freedom for prisoners," "sight for the blind," "release for the oppressed," and so on. It was His way of saying "because I have come, everything is different now."

Really?

Many people—many Christians—say that they have heard the promises of God—that He will bring forgiveness and spiritual freedom and justice and all the rest—but these good things all seem so slow in coming. Many Christians don't see that things are actually different. They don't see anything changing for the better.

That's the reason why we need to understand exactly how God works in our lives to bring about change. If we get that part wrong, we may in fact not see or experience any real change. We may be putting ourselves in entirely the wrong position to be changed.

Think again about June 6, 1944. Before D-Day, Europe had been locked up like a fortress. And then in the early morning hours, the largest naval armada in the history of the world approached the north of France through the troughs and crests of violent waves, and the Allied Forces landed and began to scratch and claw their way across beaches and up cliffs, just to get a foothold. Really, just to get one toe onto the continent. At the end of that long day, in one sense, nothing had changed.

Poland, France, Austria and Belgium were all still firmly held by the massive German war machine.

But the first step to victory was claiming one beach.

On D-Day it may have seemed that not much was different, but people with a forward-looking eye knew that *everything* was different. The tide had turned.

On an earlier occasion of victory, Winston Churchill, the prime minister of Great Britain, had said: "This is not the end. It is not even the beginning of the end. It may be the end of the beginning."[2] For us—whether we are fighting against sin, against temptations, against disease, or against compulsion or addiction—in Christ we see the victory that is the end of the beginning of the war.

I like to think of the day in the synagogue in Nazareth when Jesus made His public announcement as J-Day. It was the turning of the tide for the human race. The Anointed One had come. And He was about to get to work.

It was "J-Day" because of Jesus. But also because of "Jubilee."

The last phrase of Jesus' announcement in the synagogue, "to proclaim the year of the Lord's favor" (v. 19), was a reference to a great tradition rooted in the law of the Old Testament, whereby God commanded that the Israelites observe a great season of spiritual renewal every 50 years called "the Year of Jubilee." In that special year, a kind of super-Sabbath, the people were to return to all the essential values of God: forgiveness, justice, freedom, and much more. The Year of Jubilee was to be, for the people, a way of remembering that everything could be different. Because Yahweh was radically different from all the other gods, such as Baal and Molech—gods who were served by throngs of people mainly so that their crops would grow—the followers of Yahweh, the children of Abraham, could know that they were a different people. Not in the sense of being odd but of being rich with the promises of God.

We all need Jubilee seasons in our lives. We need (and more important, God offers us) the opportunity to say, "I need to get back to the important things, the essential things."

In this book, we will delve into seven important Jubilee truths that are all part of the idea of Jubilee, or the observance of the Year of Jubilee.

1. *Sabbath*: rehearsing that God and God alone is in control
2. *Redemption*: being freed by God's great acts of deliverance
3. *Freedom*: cherishing the liberty that God brings to every area of life
4. *Forgiveness*: accepting the mercy of God and letting go of those you've held in debt
5. *Healing*: letting God restore your spirit, your body and your relationships
6. *Justice*: standing for what is right and being an advocate for the downtrodden
7. *Proclamation*: knowing what you stand for and letting others know it

Really wise people observe and take advantage of seasons in life. Most of us cannot survive life if it goes on in one long string of days: the same old same old; the wearying, wearing, monotonous, unrelenting flow of one month into the next, one year into the next, one decade into the next. On and on until we die.

There is a better way. God gives us seasons of life for a reason. I'm glad to live in the upper Midwest of the United States where winter is winter and summer is summer. There is real snow and real heat. And the best times are often autumn and spring, when one season is giving way to the next and you pass through a metamorphosis of life.

But besides giving us the climatic seasons, God blessed us with a seasonality to life that includes a 7-day week, a 365-day year, which the Scriptures say gives us an opportunity for life to be continually changing. Monotony is not the way things are supposed to be. We are to make something special of one day of the week (the idea of Sabbath, which we come to in the next chapter). We should also mark the passing of the new year, being mindful that when we start to make one more trip around the sun, life begins again.

And then there are the spiritual seasons. The Old Testament calls them festivals, or Sabbaths. It is unfortunate that most of us live so far removed from the life of the farmer that we are unaware of the joy and sweat of the time of planting and the exuberance of the time of harvesting. Where I live we get our food from a large local grocery store that has very little "local" to it. The meats and vegetables and canned goods come to the shelves from around the country, and even other countries, and I have to remind myself of the wonder at how God takes care of me and my family. When I pray, "Give us this day our daily bread," I know that the bread is abundant—baked, sliced and wrapped in plastic—and just a minute up the road at the convenience store. But when I stop to reflect on my life, I pray the prayer and consciously think of the amazing work my Creator does with seeds and soil so that I can live.

It shouldn't take us much effort to use our imaginations to put ourselves back in Old Testament times, when an offering wasn't a personal check written out and placed in an offering tray, but a sheaf of grain, freshly cut, smelling of life, young and tender, the first cut from the field, brought as an offering to the living God. What an amazing experience it must have been to give to the Lord the first fruits of the harvest.

Yes, God gives us seasons as a gift. Because of seasons we know that God gives new beginnings. This year may have really stunk, but there is always next year. Next year always holds promise.

This was especially true in the case of the Year of Jubilee, which was a rare occurrence. Once every 50 years, which practically means once in a lifetime. So what was this special season all about? To get that answer, we go to Leviticus 25:

> Count off seven Sabbaths of years—seven times seven years—so that the seven Sabbath years amount to a period of forty-nine years. Then have the trumpet sounded everywhere on the tenth day of the seventh month; on the Day of Atonement sound the trumpet throughout your land. Consecrate the fiftieth year and proclaim liberty throughout the land to all its inhabitants. It shall be a jubilee for you; each of you is to return to his family property and each to his own clan. The fiftieth year shall be a jubilee for you; do not sow and do not reap

> what grows of itself or harvest the untended vines. For it is a jubilee and is to be holy for you; eat only what is taken directly from the fields. In this Year of Jubilee everyone is to return to his own property (vv. 8-13).

God told the children of Abraham to take one day a week and consider it a special day of rest and of coming to know Him, the Sabbath. (The Hebrew word *shavat* literally means "to stop." So a Sabbath day [in Hebrew, *Shabbat*] or a Sabbath year was a designated time for God's people to stop their day-to-day activities, to do something different.) And then, in Leviticus, God tells the people to have a Sabbath year every seven years.

Now that's a more radical idea because it included not planting the fields. What if someone told you that your employer was going to give you every seventh year off? Your next question would be, *With or without pay?* The answer in Leviticus is, "Without pay." God basically said, "Grow enough in your fields the previous years so that you can store up enough grain to last you through your sabbatical year." An interesting proposition. Sounds really good to have a year off from work every seventh year, but it does mean working quite hard the other years.

The Year of Jubilee was a "super Sabbath" year. The verses quoted above tell us about it. Not only was this a Sabbath year in which the people could get a rest from the back-breaking work of planting, cultivating and harvesting the fields, but it also was a year in which the people were to forgive their debts to each other, to release slaves so that they could return to their ancestral homes, to seek out the balance of the scales of justice, to proclaim liberty to people who were in bondage.

The Year of Jubilee was God's way of helping His people start over. It was a time to stop everything that normally happened, take a look around and set things right. To find out what belonged to whom and give it back, in a phrase coined by Walter Brueggemann.

The Year of Jubilee began in the fiftieth year on the Day of Atonement, the holiest of all the Jewish festivals—a day of contrition on which the people watched a goat wander off into the wilderness as a symbol of their sins being removed far from them. The Day of Atonement, Yom Kippur, was God's reminder to the people that the most important of all new beginnings is the freshness of forgiveness. No wonder Jesus announced the Year of Jubilee and said that He had come to fulfill it.

And we should note this, too: The Hebrew word translated into English as "jubilee" literally means "the blowing of a trumpet." In Old Testament times, trumpets were not made of brass, but of the ram's horn, the shofar. Blow through the hollow interior of the ram's horn and what comes out is a wild, mournful sound that drifts in pitch and echoes. In the book of Judges, we read that Gideon took a mere 300 soldiers, surrounded the encampment of the Midianites and Amalekites and shocked them into terror when all 300 revealed torches and let loose the arresting sound of 300 shofars. The New Testament associates the Day of Judgment with the sounding of trumpets.

We have come to use "jubilee" to describe festivities and celebrations. A city, for example, might sponsor a "jubilee" for an annual music festival. But if we stick with the original Hebrew meaning—a trumpet blast—it's easy to remember that there are times in life when God has to get our attention by a trumpet blast in the ear. That's what trumpets do: arrest attention. They pierce the noise. They dominate.

God is still trying to get our attention. "Jubilee," the "trumpet blast," is one way we can listen.

I know that if my life becomes one long blur, it won't be good for me and it won't be honoring to God. I need to stop, to experience *Shabbat*. I need to ask God to teach me again about forgiveness and redemption and liberty and justice and about all the things that really matter.

And maybe I will learn that everything really can be different.

Notes

1. Dwight D. Eisenhower, "D-Day Broadcast to the People of Western Europe: June 6, 1944." Text courtesy of the Dwight D. Eisenhower Memorial Commission. http://www.eisenhowermemorial.org/speeches/19440606%20D-Day%20broadcast%20to%20people%20of%20Western%20Europe.htm (accessed May 2008).
2. Winston Churchill, from a speech given at the Lord Mayor's Luncheon following the victory at El Alameinin, North Africa, in London, November 10, 1942. Text courtesy of The Churchill Centre. http://www.winstonchurchill.org/i4a/pages/index.cfm?pageid=388#not_the_end (accessed May 2008).

WEEK 1

SABBATH

Rehearsing that God and God Alone Is in Control

I will never forget the day that Olga Feinberg was baptized in our church, at the age of 100. Remarkably, Olga became a believer in Christ at the age of 98. She certainly knew about Christ before that, but there was no personal relationship, no real faith. She knew it, and others in her life knew it, too. She had a reputation for being rather difficult long before she began the final decades of her life. Her bristly personality rubbed other people the wrong way. Her niece was one of only a handful of people who hung in there with her, telling her of God's love as Olga moved into the final years of her life.

As Olga told the story, one night she became powerfully aware of the presence of God, and heard Jesus calling out to her, extending Himself to her. She realized then, at 98, that she really was alone without God, and that life could be better than it had been before. Like so many others, Olga's faith step was one of relinquishing her life into the arms of God—of letting go, and letting God get hold of her.

In the months that followed, Olga went through a genuine transformation, a fact that still amuses me whenever I think of all the experts on human behavior who say that people don't really change much after age 20 or so. Olga *did* change. And she told people about the grace of Christ almost up to her dying day. She actually made it to 104 and a half (you count half-years when you are less than 10 or more than 100), and then her body was done.

Thinking about Olga always reminds me of Hebrews 4:9-10, which says, "There remains, then, a Sabbath-rest for the people of God; for anyone who enters God's rest also rests from his own work, just as God did from his."

Rest in peace, Olga.

The God Who Stops

From beginning to end, the Bible talks about rest and work, which should compel us to search its pages for wisdom; there is hardly a person on earth who does not wrestle with balancing work and rest. Do any of these questions sound familiar?

1. How did I get into a situation in which life seems like a treadmill that I'm running on but not getting anywhere?

2. I used to like my work, but now it just seems like drudgery. What happened?

3. It seems like all of my time gets grabbed by other people and other activities. How can I get back some control?

4. Life has become a blur, and I feel like I'm always running from one thing to the next. Is there some way for me to break the cycle?

5. I don't know what it means to "give God" my time and energy. Does that just mean going to church, or is there something larger I should be aiming at?

Some people and some societies deal with these kinds of issues more than others. I remember an African acquaintance telling me, "You Westerners have watches on your wrists and no time in your life; we Africans have no watches on our wrists and all the time in the world!" Cultural differences considered, it's interesting that 3,500 years ago when the laws of the Old Testament were emerging, God stipulated principles of lifestyle and pace that apply equally to the farmer in ancient Hebron as to the business executive, the college student and the homemaker of today. Human nature does not change—and neither does the principle of balancing work and rest.

Some people may, with good reason, wonder why the principle of Sabbath should be carried forward today. Doesn't the New Testament say that we live in a new era now, that the Old Testament law doesn't apply anymore? Doesn't it warn that we run the risk of losing spiritual freedom if we place ourselves under an Old Testament law like Sabbath?

These are good questions. The purpose of this chapter is to show how the principle of Sabbath—ceasing—is a universal and timeless life principle woven into Creation itself; it is not, for the Christian, a law. As we'll see, it is the idea of "change of pace" and "taking a break," but far more importantly, having times when we realize afresh that God and God alone is in control of life.

Over the centuries, Christians have responded to the Old Testament idea of Sabbath in at least three different ways:

1. Sabbath is part of the Old Testament law and has no ongoing relevance.

2. Sabbath is at the heart of Old Covenant law, which carries over to the New Covenant era (it is, after all, one of the Ten Commandments). Sunday is to Christians what Saturday was to Jews, and thus Christians should have a no-work rule on Sundays.

3. The principle of Sabbath carries over into our lives now, but that does not mean that Sunday has become the new Sabbath day.

The first view, that Sabbath belongs to a different time and place, has been the assumption of many Christians over the centuries. They would find it odd and even dangerously legalistic to carry into the Christian era a lot of rules and regulations about what one may or may not do on one day of the week.

The second view, that Sunday is the Christian Sabbath, was strongly emphasized by the Puritans in England in the seventeenth century, and so passed into many of the American Christian streams of thought. Some Americans of an older generation can still remember "blue laws" in the U.S., under which businesses, restaurants, and the like were required by law to close on Sunday, "the Sabbath." (Most of those laws have disappeared now, and it could be argued that we have lost something now that Sundays have become one more work day, one more highly scheduled day when individuals and families rush from one activity to the next.) *Chariots of Fire* won Best Picture at the Academy Awards in 1981, in part because of the compelling real-life story of Olympic runner Eric Liddell who refused to run an Olympic race on Sunday, the Sabbath, in the summer games of 1924. He stood for his principle (rooted in Scottish Presbyterianism) and garnered the admiration of millions. (In spite of the popularity of *Chariots of Fire* and widespread admiration for Liddell, there were few people who quit their soccer leagues and stopped watching sports on TV on Sundays after seeing it.)

The third view, the attempt to carry the Sabbath principle forward into our lives without bringing a lot of rules with it, has much merit. It allows us to say, "Yes, we should not ignore the fact that Sabbath is one of the Ten Commandments. Yes, it does make sense that God would command a certain rhythm in our lives. Yes, it makes sense that God would require 'holy' times in our lives so that the sacred can transform the ordinary."

So, is there a way to preserve the truth and power of Sabbath? There is, if we understand it, and if we commit to it.

Sabbath is like a prism out of which emerge many colors of truth. Taken together, the truths of Sabbath are *a time and an attitude in which we rehearse that God and God alone is in control.* That's what can happen when we cease what we normally do, take a break, pay closer attention to our Creator and then move on in life.

As we saw in the Introduction, the Hebrew word *shavat* literally means "to cease." It means taking time to get your nose out of your normal work and doing something that restores your life. It means committing to a time of devotion and worship when you tune out all the noise, all the conflict, all the people shouting their opinions at you, and really hear God speak. A weekly pattern of *Shabbat* is a great place to start, but *Shabbat* can also be a daily practice as we take short breaks from the clutter of everyday life. We can also have annual times of *Shabbat* or even once every few years, as with the Year of Jubilee—a year-long change of pace, observed every 50 years.

Sabbath and the Created Order of All Things

We call the universe in which we live the *cosmos*, a word that means "order." This term betrays a timeless truth about human beings: No matter how disordered and chaotic life becomes, we hope that somehow things will straighten out, that things turned upside down in our lives will be turned right side up, that someone will finally make things the way they were meant to be. And because God created the cosmos, most people know deep down inside that it will take the power of God to fix "the order."

Now, there are several principles of life that appear to be woven into the created order of the cosmos. We learn about them in the opening pages of Scripture. Genesis speaks of creation, and of the incredible diversity and unity of the whole as it issued from the will and word of God. Marriage, likewise, is woven into the created order, and like the united diversity of the broader creation, is a union of two very diverse genders out of which come new generations. Similarly, Sabbath is part of the created order. First word of the idea comes in Genesis 2:2: "By the seventh day God had finished the work he had been doing; so on the seventh day he rested from all his work." Later, the pattern of God's creation was set out for the human race in the law given at Mt. Sinai and summarized in the "Ten Words," or Ten Commandments, which include:

> Remember the Sabbath day by keeping it holy. Six days you shall labor and do all your work, but the seventh day is a Sabbath to the LORD your God. On it you shall not do any work, neither you, nor your son or daughter, nor your manservant or maidservant, nor your animals, nor the alien within your gates. For in six days the LORD made the heavens and the earth, the sea, and all that is in them, but he rested on the seventh day. Therefore the LORD blessed the Sabbath day and made it holy (Exodus 20:8-11).

So, how does the command to "remember the Sabbath day" carry over to our days? There must be something extraordinarily important here for God's command to be so strong. There must be something that carries over to our time . . . even if we're not farmers or sheep herders.

"Remember" points to a time of observance. We all know that if we want to let the significance of a day really impact us, we have to be intentional about observing it. My wife and I often comment in early June that we're not particularly good at observing our wedding anniversary on June 7. There is no one telling us we should observe our anniversary. There is no external necessity; it's not a matter of right or wrong. But we know that when we are intentional about stepping away from our normal busyness, when we go out for the evening and remember the significance of this date in our history, it's a good thing.

Far too often we say, "This is not a good time, we're far too busy, let's do something to celebrate sometime soon." But "sometime" never seems to come.

For the children of Abraham, the *way* to remember is specific and concrete: no plowing, no harvesting, no building. The law in Leviticus is full of detailed Sabbath regulations: Don't cook. Don't plow the fields. Don't travel. (To put it more positively: Take a break from cooking, from plowing, from traveling. Take time to do something different. *Remember*.)

In Sabbath, two principles are remembered: a time of rest, and a time that is "holy" and "blessed." In other words, we shift our attention and focus intentionally toward God, and we become more fully God-aware. First let's look first at remembering to *rest*.

All embodied creatures have a natural time of rest every day. We fall asleep, the body still, the conscious mind shut down for hours—an amazing phenomenon, really. (When we experience insomnia and try to live life without proper rest, the importance of sleep is immediately apparent.) But in addition to our daily rest, we are also designed for a weekly change of pace. In ancient times (as it still is for practicing Jews), Sabbath was an entire day of rest for everyone: men and women, boys and girls, household servants, and even the temporary immigrant. They all stopped their work to do something different.

Exodus 20 puts it this way: Because God rested, we must rest. But what does that mean? Was God utterly exhausted from creating the universe? Did creating humanity put Him over the edge? Did God sweat and strain and collapse on the weekend? Was God a candidate for a seminar in stress management?

Was creating the universe terribly taxing on Him? Or maybe the real effort was in creating the planets: bringing together just the right amount of matter, cooling it down and bringing about life. Was it difficult for God to create humanity? Was it then that God sat back and said, "I'm exhausted"?

Of course, that's not the sense we get from Genesis. It is more like this: God did His work of creation, and then He created some more, and at a certain point He said, "There. That's that. I've completed what I set out to do. Sun, moon, planet, rain, jungle, mammal, fish, human. Here is My masterpiece. And now I will do something different."

The second principle of Sabbath, after remembering to rest, is observing a time that is blessed and holy. The word "holy" in Scripture means "different" or "set aside for a special purpose." The Temple was a holy place and even had holy furnishings: candlesticks and tables and curtains that had a special purpose, a function different from the everyday versions of the same items. Likewise, God's people are called holy in the sense that they have a specially designated purpose in the world.

Knowing the difference between ordinary things in life and the specially consecrated things must be part of our basic spiritual awareness. It is not surprising, then, that some Christians over the centuries have looked to the first day of the week, Sunday, as a natural time to play out the Sabbath principle. Going back to the first and second centuries, Christians gathered for worship on Sundays (rather than on the Jewish Sabbath, Saturday) because Sunday was the day of Jesus' resurrection. Worshiping on a different day is not wrong. Worship, as defined in the New Testament, should be a daily experience of making oneself a living sacrifice to God—it should never be limited to one day of the week (see Romans 12:1). But to the earliest Christians, Sundays just seemed to make sense for their worship gatherings, and all over the world and across the centuries, other Christians have followed their lead.

There is no question about it: When we gather for worship as a regular weekly pattern, following the outline that goes back to the ancient synagogues—praise, word, prayer—and have this different, "holy" part of our week, we are shaped and filled and connected. (Unless we're worshiping in a toxic environment or in a church that has gotten worship twisted out of shape.) All patterns of life have a shaping influence. Smoke every day and your lungs will turn grey. Exercise every day and your muscles become firm. Read the Bible every day and your mind is filled with God-thoughts. Pray numerous times a day and you gain a continual awareness of the presence of God. Worship once a week with a congregation of believers and you build a pattern of ceasing (*Shabbat*) what you normally do in order to serve God in the submission of worship.

One of the reasons the Scriptures are so strong on commanding that we be intentional about these "different" days of our weeks is that God knows there is a riptide pulling us into a chaotic ocean of activity that will eventually drown us. In his bestselling book *Margin: Restoring Emotional, Physical, Financial, and Time Reserves to Overloaded Lives*, author Richard A. Swenson, MD, writes this about the cultural currents of modern America:

> The manner in which progress evolves, therefore, ALWAYS results in more and more of everything faster

> and faster. . . . The profusion of progress is on a collision course with human limits. Once the threshold of these limits is exceeded, overload displaces margin. . . . [P]rogress is not evil. Similarly, stress, change, complexity, speed, intensity and overload are, for the most part, not enemies. But we have different conditions at play than at any other time in our history. . . . Our relationships are being starved to death by velocity. No one has the time to listen, let alone love. Our children lay wounded on the ground, run over by our high-speed good intentions. Is God now pro-exhaustion? Doesn't He lead people beside still waters anymore? Who plundered those wide-open spaces of the past, and how can we get them back?[1]

One solution to the dilemma that Swenson raises surely is Sabbath.

In his excellent book *The Rest of God: Restoring Your Soul by Restoring Sabbath*, pastor and author Mark Buchanan says that there are two dimensions to Sabbath: Sabbath day and Sabbath attitude.[2] Sabbath *day* is the day each week that we set aside to rest and turn our focus to God. Sabbath *attitude* is a disposition toward life that is more liberating and transforming and healing than anything else we can do, because we are rehearsing the truth that God and God alone is in control.

It is far too easy for us to think that we control life. Even in times that are obviously out of our control—a time of illness, losing a job, a broken engagement, recovering from an accident—we easily become obsessed with doing everything that can possibly be done, chasing solutions for situations that have no solution but faith, patience and perseverance. We need times when we say, "Okay, I'm not going to try to control the world today. I need to remember that God and God alone is in control." That is the Sabbath attitude that happens when we cease. Stop. *Shavat.* Change the pace.

I know how desperately I need to keep coming back to that truth. I work in a Christian organization, a church. One would think that in a church, the leaders know and live in the essential truths of life, including the reality that God and God alone is in control. But I find myself continually having to relearn that the welfare of the church I serve doesn't rest on my shoulders, that I am not the genesis of the really bright ideas, that my calling is not to keep as many people as possible happy. There is something inside me that makes me want to control things, which is a frightening thought—taking control is stepping into God's domain. As Buchanan says in *The Rest of God*:

> [W]e mimic God in order to remember we're not God. In fact, that is a good definition of Sabbath, imitating God so that we stop trying to be God. . . . Sabbath-keeping involves a recognition of our own weakness and smallness, that we are made from dust, that we hold our treasures in clay jars, and that without proper care we break.[3]

Lord of the Sabbath

At the start of Jesus' public ministry, there in that synagogue in Nazareth, He announced that the "year of the Lord's favor," the culmination of Jubilee, was being fulfilled from that day on. In that trumpet blast, Jesus asserted that going forward, everything would be different. Those who heard Him make those astonishing claims of redemption, forgiveness and healing on that day and in the following years of His ministry should have known that things *can* be different. They should have known because God had His people rehearsing the truth of "differentness" (holiness) for centuries through the simple practice of the holy day.

Frequently in Jesus' teaching ministry, Sabbath became a point of dispute with His listeners—in particular, with the religious leaders of the day. They had a lot at stake in their definition of Sabbath. Over many years, they had built up hundreds of regulations and standards to define the proper observance of Sabbath. There were rules about clothing, eating, hunting, tying knots, traveling, how much you could carry and what was too much to carry.

Now, there are problems with all bureaucratic systems. First, they take on a life of their own, needing to be scrupulously maintained and elaborated on further. The roles of the scribes and religious lawyers in Jesus' day emerged out of the need to interpret and enforce the Sabbath regulations. The second problem is that legalistic systems become more like fortresses than palaces. The law of God should be a structure people can live and flourish in, not a walled city focusing on who is in and who is out.

That kind of stifling restriction had become commonplace and nearly unbearable for many of God's people in Jesus' day: Maintenance of the structure had become more important to the religious leaders than the health of the people inside. And that's why—incredibly—the "experts in the law" objected so vociferously when Jesus healed someone with a withered hand (see Luke 6:6-11) and someone who was blind (see John 9) on the Sabbath. One might easily read the accounts of those arguments without stopping to consider how outrageous their objections were. But imagine that you witness the healing of someone you love by the power of the Good Shepherd, and then the religious authorities tell you that such a miracle should not happen on a particular day of the week. It goes beyond wrongheadedness; it is a sobering picture of how deluded any of us can become when our religion becomes a system that obstructs the very goal it was created to reach.

Here's where the stories of those Sabbath healings get interesting: Jesus' response to the grossly misguided leaders was simple, clear and radical. Referring to Himself, He said, "The Son of Man is Lord of the Sabbath" (Luke 6:5). We can barely imagine the magnitude of what Jesus was claiming, but think of it this way: A political candidate today says that he or she is not going to pay federal income taxes because he or she is above the law. That person would be considered not just wrong, but crazy! Who would dare make a claim in public that he or she stood above the law?

That is, roughly, what Jesus was saying. Of course, His claim was perfectly logical if He was actually the co-Creator with God the Father of everything that exists—including the human race and the patterns of life healthy for the human race. Including the Sabbath.

Jesus' answer helps us in several ways. When I think of Jesus Christ as Lord of the Sabbath, then I know that if I'm trying to follow Him, I need to take Sabbath seriously—and on His terms. What does it matter what a church or denomination says "Sabbath" means if it is not directly connected to the intent of the

Lord of the Sabbath? In the life of Jesus, we see a natural and normal observance of Sabbath. He went week by week to the synagogue on the seventh day. He changed the pace of His life and ministry, frequently withdrawing from the crowd and His work to quiet, alone places where He communicated with God the Father.

Knowing Jesus as Lord of Sabbath reminds me that all of the spiritual patterns of my life—serving, devotion, worship, rest—should enhance my connection with Him. If they don't, then I may have built those patterns on false grounds. I need to remind myself that I am always one short step away from constructing my own arbitrary, self-authenticating (and pointless) system, just like the religious leaders of Jesus' day.

The Sabbath principle should not add confusion, but help to settle the complexity of our lives. We are called to persevere in our normal calling in life and then cease, open our eyes, ask God to speak into our lives, do something different for a day or for a season, and come out with a stronger sense of His Lordship over all of life. When we hear—*really* hear—Jesus saying, "I am Lord of Sabbath," then we receive the enormous blessing of coming under His spiritual direction—pure, unambiguous, simple. If, on the other hand, we make *ourselves* Sabbath lords or worship lords or personal Bible study lords or prayer lords, then the inversion of lordship will empty our lives of power and hope.

Sabbath Made for Us

Jesus called Himself "the Lord of the Sabbath," but here is an equally arresting claim: Jesus told the religious experts that "the Sabbath was made for man, not man for the Sabbath" (Mark 2:27).

As it was in Jesus' day, Galilee, in the north of Israel, is fertile and lush. Fields of grain wave in the wind, promising new life at harvest time. One Sabbath day, Jesus, His disciples and other stragglers were walking a path that wound its way through the fields. As they walked, a few of Jesus' followers picked some heads of grain and popped them in their mouths, enjoying the nourishing freshness, listening as Jesus talked.

The religious experts, whose intent was to pile up every accusation they could possibly make against Jesus, objected that His followers were breaking the Sabbath—they were "harvesting." Now, a common-sense interpretation of the Levitical law is that God commanded farmers to take a day of the week when they set their plows and scythes and pitchforks aside, let the oxen graze and *rest*. Be renewed. Calling Jesus' disciples' grabbing a few heads of grain and shelling them between their hands for a snack "harvesting" is a pretty big stretch—unless you're a religious legalist. Unless you want to construct a system of rules so binding that only an elite few—"the righteous"—can follow them.

Jesus took action to expose the self-righteousness of the spiritual elite. At turn after turn, He pointed people to the *spirit* of the law, and on that day amid the fields that were reminders of God's rich blessings in life, Jesus said this: "The Sabbath was made for man, not man for the Sabbath." What may seem like common sense to us was an absolutely out-of-the-box idea for the Pharisees and other religious leaders. Jesus turned right side up what had been turned upside down—though to the

Pharisees it looked like He was capsizing the boat, sure to sink the whole thing and drown many.

Sabbath is God's gift to us, not a maze through which God is running us like lab rats. The "stop principle" was never meant to be an imposition, but divine permission.

Because, as history shows, to cease is sometimes the hardest thing for us to do.

We don't know how good the ancient Israelites were at observing Sabbath. We don't know if they actually obeyed (and received the blessing) of the Year of Jubilee.

And in the twenty-first century, ceasing is 10 times harder. If you stop, you may not make as much money. If you intend to stop, you have to think ahead. If you stop, others may criticize you for gumming up the works, for not doing things they want you to do, for just being different. People will always ask you to do more for them; they will hardly ever ask you to stop and take a break (except for really wise people who understand the Sabbath principle).

I know the owner of a store who decided years ago that he would keep it a six-day-a-week operation, closed all day Sunday. He knew that conventional wisdom said to stay open seven days a week. Sell, sell, sell. Make more money. Increase the margin. But this God-loving businessman decided to follow the principle of ceasing.

The national corporate office told him he was crazy, and pleaded with him to run seven days a week, but he stuck to his guns. And over the passage of time, his store was among the most profitable outlets in the whole company. That made the big bosses stand up and notice. It didn't surprise this man, however. He believed that things woven into the created order of things will always bring more rewards.

The Sabbath principle was made for us; we were not made for it. God wants to gift our lives with variation and renewal and rhythm. For then we are able to gift God with a life of worship.

Ten Ways to Develop a Sabbath Attitude

If our work lives require intentionality, dedication and discipline, it is no less true of working the Sabbath principle into the flow of our lives. To get you started, here are 10 ways you can be intentional about developing a life-changing Sabbath attitude:

1. Decide What Day Will Be Your Sabbath

Determine one day a week to be your "change of pace," a time to back off from trying to control every detail of life, a time to remember that God and God alone is in control. You may think right away of the weekend as that designated time and figure that *Shabbat* is already a part of the pattern of your life—and that may be partly true. But most of us can do better than coming to Friday and thinking, *Let's see . . . tomorrow we'll get some yard work done, then we'll catch the ball game in the afternoon. Sunday we'll slog on over to church, get that done, get a quick lunch before we scatter and then get the kids to do their homework in the evening.* This scenario is not a change of pace. At the end of the weekend can we honestly say that we are refreshed, recharged, reconnected with God and better prepared to move out into a new week? If not, genuine *Shabbat* has not happened, and perhaps another day of the week or a different approach to the weekend should be considered.

2. Rest in Ways that Restore

If you "change your pace" by doing something more frenetic and draining than what you do during the rest of your week, you are digging yourself into a hole. Be wise about your rest. Choose to do things that restore your body, spirit and relationships. If you live in a household with other family members, ask yourself whether the result of your Sabbath time results in a stronger bond within your family.

We can't be overly idealistic about this, of course. You don't achieve family harmony by way of legislation any more than the Pharisees got closer to God through their considerable rules and regulations. But we can be intentional about setting up conditions in which family members have time to reconnect with each other.

3. Worship in a Christian Community Every Week

The long history of worship on a given day of the week has its high points and low points, but when churches understand the purpose of worship—to serve God with praise in song, to listen to God's Word, to bring offerings, to share in the Lord's Supper—when worship is a weekly pattern of life, God shapes our thoughts and attitudes in ways we may not even be aware of. Worship is the submission of the whole self to God. We walk away from worship more aware of our humble but honored place in the universe. We realize that we are not God, and that we wear ourselves out trying to control what cannot be controlled. And we remember that we have to go back out into the world and carry out our responsibilities, whatever they may be, as if we are working directly for God.

4. Preserve Worship as a "Holy" and "Blessed" Pattern of Life

When we gather for worship, we're doing something "holy," which means out-of-the-ordinary, different. Worship should never be ho-hum. It is not a nice and friendly get-together. It is a time when revolutionaries gather together to receive their marching orders from the Lord and Master of the universe and then spread out in a campaign that is not destructive, but life-giving. Worship is an act of subversion against the pockets of evil in the world. Worship is holy. Leland Ryken, professor at Wheaton College, wrote, "[S]omeone claimed that we work at our play and play at our work. Today the confusion has deepened: we worship our work, work at our play, and play at our worship."[4] When we refuse to succumb to that destructive model and instead live in rhythm with the Sabbath pattern, our day of worship is a "blessed" day.

5. Commit to a Quiet Time of Devotion Every Day

Engage daily with God in Scripture and prayer. Sabbath is not just a weekly pattern. We can and should seek occasional seasons of Sabbath when we come back to the essential realities of the Christ-life—a Jubilee season. But "ceasing" is also part of pacing every day. If you wake up in the morning with the alarm blaring, get washed and dressed with your brain churning away at the lists of things to accomplish that day—already sensing, as a knot tightens in your stomach, that you're probably not going to pull it off—you've started the day on the wrong foot. If you end the day in a stupor, disinterested in everybody, ready to collapse, not having had hardly a thought of God at any time—that is a toxic day, especially if that's the way you continue in the days that follow. A daily pattern of *Shabbat* includes time to pray, time to read from Scripture and time to meditate on it (important because just reading Scripture and slamming the pages shut with no cultivated thought, no rumination, is not a biblical understanding of listening to the voice of God). There is no substitute for a "quiet time" each day, a time of devotion . . . no matter the length of time! Better to have just 10 minutes most days than to commit to an hour each day and never get around to it.

6. Determine to Live More Simply

That's simple right? Not necessarily. Most people would like to simplify their lives—to get less junk mail, to have fewer machines like lawn mowers and snow blowers and cars that demand we serve them by feeding them oil and gas and cleaning their insides. Computers and the Internet are great . . . when they do what we want them to do. (I admit that I've had days when I've been convinced that the computer on my desk is dangling me like a puppet on a string, laughing at my frustration, tantalizing me like a hypnotist swinging his watch slowly in front of my eyes.) The "simpler" life gets with all the modern inventions of convenience, the more complicated it becomes. And we end up having a harder and harder time hearing the trumpet call of God, the arresting command that says, "Stop! Look around at what your life has become. Look at Me."

What does that mean for you? Walking or riding a bike instead of driving to certain destinations? Turning off your cell phone at times you've designated for Sabbath? Taking a month-long fast from shopping, except for groceries? Reading email only once a day? Unsubscribing from magazines that don't enrich your life? The possibilities are endless. Think of your week as a blank canvas. Now what do you choose to put there?

7. Redefine "Success" in God's Terms

Refuse to become a slave of avarice. In my dictionary, the first definition of "success" is "the accomplishment of a purpose," and the second is "the attainment of popularity or profit." Now, in God's terms, there is nothing wrong with popularity or profit, but they are only sometimes the byproduct of real success. Much of the time, success as "the accomplishment of a purpose" draws little popularity or profit. Can you live with that? Can you do the right thing, even if there are no thanks and no pay or applause that come with it? When you choose Sabbath, you are committing to break the normal patterns of your life in order to focus on God—and that may mean making less money because you choose to step back from your money-making work. You may have heard a really "successful" person claim, "I haven't taken a vacation in 10 years." Is that really something to brag about? Would that person's children applaud? There is no better measure of real success than Jesus' words, "Well done, good and faithful servant."

8. Open Up Margins in Your Life

Have time that is unplanned, unscheduled and uncommitted. We sometimes prevent good things from happening in our lives (the spontaneous luncheon, the unexpected invitation to attend a sporting event, the unplanned wrestling match with the kids) because there is no margin. When my daughter returned from spending half her summer overseas just last week, I was glad that I had kept my schedule flexible because she was available for a cup of coffee or to have lunch at odd hours during the day, usually with little advance notice. What a shame if we are so locked in that we can never do anything on the spur of the moment. Taking delight in the random encounters that come our way is a wonderful reminder that God is in control.

9. Use Constructive Stress, Minimize Destructive Stress

It is not true that we can or should avoid all stress. Constructive stress is when we apply our energies in ways that stretch us so that we learn new things, try new things, do things outside of our comfort zones. But destructive stress is when we get stuck in a perpetual state of tension arising from things like insecurity, fear, greed or running from people and issues in life that we will have to face sooner or later. The Sabbath principle is the best stress-reliever we have, because "rehearsing the truth that God and God alone is in control" frees us from thinking we are God, a job for which we never should apply.

10. Make a Plan to Have a Special Jubilee in Your Life

It is important to set good daily and weekly patterns, but as was the case with the children of Israel, everyone needs an occasional longer season in life to significantly change their posture and pace of life. To come back to God in a significant new way. You may not be able to get three months off work—though if your line of work does allow some form of sabbatical, don't ignore it!—but anyone can say, "I sense God is sounding His trumpet in my life, trying to get my attention, telling me to stop and be filled by Him. I know I need to do this. I know I've needed to for a long time. I know that if I don't, I will end up shrinking away, and that does not honor God." Why not add a spiritual facet to this year's summer vacation? Or take one day a month to be alone, read God's Word and pray. Or decide that this year you will cut the amount of time you watch TV in half and instead spend an hour each day in prayer, reading Scripture and listening to God's voice. Get creative! Ask God to blow the trumpet.

If there is a real hesitation to change the posture of your life for a season, consider this story:

> One day a woodsman challenged a fellow woodsman to an all-day wood-chopping contest. The first man labored heavily, stopping only for a brief lunch, whereas the other man took a leisurely lunch and several breaks throughout the day. The first man was shocked and annoyed at the end of the day to find that the other man had chopped much more wood than he had. "I don't get it," he said. "Every time I checked, you were taking a rest, yet you chopped more wood than I did."
>
> "What you didn't notice," said the winning woodsman, "is that every time I sat down to rest, I was sharpening my ax."

Notes

1. Richard A. Swenson, MD, *Margin: Restoring Emotional, Physical, Financial, and Time Reserves to Overloaded Lives* (Colorado Springs, CO: Navpress Publishing Group, 1995), p. 155.
2. Mark Buchanan, *The Rest of God: Restoring Your Soul by Restoring Sabbath* (Nashville, TN: Thomas Nelson, 2006).
3. Ibid., p. 87.
4. Leland Ryken, *Redeeming the Time: A Christian Approach to Work and Leisure* (Grand Rapids, MI: Baker Books, 1995), p. 50.

WEEK 1

DAILY REFLECTIONS

Day 1

Consecrate the fiftieth year and proclaim liberty throughout the land to all its inhabitants. It shall be a jubilee for you.

LEVITICUS 25:10

We all need seasons in life when we come back to the first things, the central truths, the top priorities. That's what all the different kinds of Sabbath did for God's people in the Old Testament. Jubilee was celebrated once every 50 years as a God-instituted opportunity for people to really stop, look at the compass of their lives and see what direction they were going.

Jubilee—the sounding of the trumpet—is when God arrests our attention. It is a time when God can get us to stop doing the petty things, the temporary things, the things that won't last, so that we can learn again about life lived for eternity. Jubilee is a time to "proclaim liberty" because God's work frees us from all bondage to practice rest. It is a time to be restored and evaluate our work, to heal from wounds of the past, and to make a new commitment to justice. It is these themes and others that will be our focus in the seven weeks of this 50-day spiritual journey.

Make It Real: Take five minutes sometime today to read Leviticus 25:8-31. Don't worry if some of the concepts seem strange now. Just pray to God that He will use these 50 days in your life to challenge, to heal and to direct your ways. Decide now when and where each day you will cease your activities and meet with Him.

Day 2

By the seventh day God had finished the work he had been doing; so on the seventh day he rested from all his work.

GENESIS 2:2

A University of Chicago medical study has shown a link between sleep deprivation and obesity. Other research shows that teens put themselves at risk for cognitive and emotional difficulties, poor grades and accidents if they deprive themselves of sleep. What can we learn from this? When we try to burn the candle at both ends, we end up burned.

The Hebrew word *shavat* (from which we get the English word Sabbath) literally means to cease. To stop what you are doing. To end one thing so that something else can happen. God did not *shavat* on the seventh day because He was exhausted to the point of collapse. He stopped because He was finished with what He intended to do, and was ready to do other things (such as taking care of this incredible world He had created).

And so a pattern was set for the whole universe. All of life would spin in cycles. Day gives way to night, and then night is broken by the dawn. We loop around the sun. Dry spells last for a season. Spring keeps coming. We sleep regularly, and usually at night. Every day is a new beginning.

One of the commands of God—a most serious command, repeated as much as any other command in the Old Testament—is that we choose to practice *Shabbat*. To stop. Not a rolling stop like a novice driver slinking past a stop sign, but a full stop. God stopped what He was doing and let His glorious creation shine. And He invites us to do the same.

Make It Real: Find half an hour sometime today to stop all your normal activity. Go to some restful place and think through what God has created in your life. Give thanks to God and tell Him what parts of your life could use a rest at this time.

Day 3

And God blessed the seventh day and made it holy,
because on it he rested from all his work.

GENESIS 2:3

How would you respond if someone were to ask you, "What was the most special day in your life?" Maybe it was graduation day, or a wedding day, or the day when your first child was born. Maybe it was the first time you traveled to an ocean or to a mountain range. Maybe the day you gave your life to God and took a step of faith from which there was no turning back.

God knows that all of us need more than one "special day" in our lives, so He established the idea of a cyclical special day called the Sabbath. He called this day "holy," which means "set aside for a special purpose." God wants each of us to have a blessed day—and doesn't that sound good? To have a day—not just a once-in-a-lifetime day but a regular day, a once-a-week day—when we cease what we normally do and do something different in order to connect with God. To connect with the important people in our lives. To disconnect from the busy, frenetic, competitive, tension-filled "normal" days. How long ago did we forget that God built this holy time into Creation itself?

For some people, the seventh day works out to be a real *Shabbat*, but for some it's a different day of the week. They stay away from the office, do special things with the family and reconnect with their home, and add their voice to a time of worship with a gathered people, whether on Saturday night or Sunday morning or night. They regularly observe a holy time in their week. No matter the day, it is a time when they say, "God, please do something different today. Please give me rest from my work. Please restore my body, heart and soul. Please bless this day in a way that changes all of my days."

Make It Real: Sometime today, sit down with your calendar and think about what day during the week could be a different, "holy" day for you on a regular basis. Would it be Sunday? Saturday? Another day? Think it through and discuss with your family members if you live with family. Make some lists: What activities could you avoid doing on this special day? What special things could you intentionally do? And then ask yourself this challenging question: *What are the barriers I would have to overcome to make this happen?*

Day 4

There remains, then, a Sabbath-rest for the people of God; for anyone who enters God's rest also rests from his own work, just as God did from his. Let us, therefore, make every effort to enter that rest, so that no one will fall by following in their example of disobedience.

HEBREWS 4:9-11

It's Sunday morning. A pastor goes to the lectern in front of his church in Lancashire, England, opens a document with the peculiar title "The Declaration of Sports," and begins to read. He reads reluctantly because he thinks the document is ridiculous, yet he has no choice in the matter—King James I of England has commanded it be read in all the churches. The same king who sponsored the translation of the *King James Version* of the Bible is in a petty tug-of-war with the Puritans over what Christians can or cannot do on Sundays. While the Puritans are legalistically restrictive, James's Declaration of Sports says that in good conscience, believers can dance, leap, engage in sports and drink ale on Sundays.

We don't do well when we try to make the idea of Sabbath about regulations. The principle carried over from the Old Testament to the New Testament (and so to our era) is that it is wise to have a special day during the week when we cease regular activities so we can worship God and connect with God and the important people in our lives. But Sabbath is not only a day of the week; it is also an *attitude* that we carry with us every single day, an attitude of acknowledgment that God and God alone is in control.

That may seem like a simple proposition and one that we already know well. But the truth is that we do *not* know it well. We are continually trying to control more things in life than we are able. We think we know more than we do. We are most comfortable in environments where we control the temperature, the lighting, the surroundings.

When God says, "*Shabbat!*" He is saying, "Stop and remember that I am God and you are not." Trust it. Believe it. Rest in it. Rehearsing that truth will do more to revolutionize our lives than making laws about what we can or cannot do on Sundays.

Make It Real: Make two columns on a piece of paper and write "Things I can do" at the top of one and "Things only God can do" at the top of the other. Then list particular things in the next 24 hours that fit each of these categories. Pray for God to bring a "Sabbath attitude" as you begin to acknowledge His control.

Day 5

Remember the Sabbath day by keeping it holy, as the Lord your God has commanded you. Six days you shall labor and do all your work, but the seventh day is a Sabbath to the Lord your God.

EXODUS 20:8-9

From time to time, someone questions why we have seven days in a week—they think an alternative might be better.

They tried a 10-day week in France. It was 1792, and the National Convention of the French Revolution adopted a 10-day week with 10-hour days. Ignoring Judeo-Christian tradition, they proposed that this more rational way of keeping time would make people happier and more productive. It didn't work.

Neither did Stalin's six-day week, which conveniently discarded the seventh, religiously oriented day. (In Russia, the

Christian holy day, the first day of the week, is called *Voskresenye*, "Resurrection.")

It seems as though the seven-day week is not just an arbitrary number, but a pattern written into creation itself. And so people say, "The weekend is just around the corner" and "Thank God it's Friday."

Thank God, indeed. It is good to work, good to be productive, and it is good to stop and do something else. When the Israelites escaped the bondage of Egypt into the freedom and the challenge of the wilderness, God gave them, through Moses, 10 life-giving words. We know them as the Ten Commandments, and toward the top of the list is the command to "remember" or "observe" a day in the week when we stop (*shavat*) what we normally do and do something different, something holy. (And that day makes the rest of the days more holy, as well.)

What does your week look like? Does it have productivity, not mere activity? Does it include time with the important people in your life and also time alone when you can think, reflect and pray? Does it have a time when you worship? Such things happen when we choose to make them happen. This is why God said, "Remember!"

Make It Real: Sit down sometime today and list the seven days of the week. Write one thing on each day that could be and should be different in your life pattern. It may be when you go to bed, when you rise, when you have family time or when you watch television. Ask yourself, *How can I be more intentional and less wasteful with the time God gives me?*

Day 6

Be still, and know that I am God; I will be exalted among the nations, I will be exalted in the earth.

PSALM 46:10

It was one of the harshest winters in memory in the Ardennes, and one of the most intense battles of World War II. Later they called it the "Battle of the Bulge," because the German offensive took Allied forces completely by surprise. In the end, however, the line held–it only bulged in the middle.

On Christmas Day, General McAuliffe's men were hunkered down in the town of Bastogne, Belgium, completely encircled by German troops. They had been besieged by 17 different assaults on the town and bombed relentlessly. But when presented with the option of surrendering by German envoys, General McAuliffe's response was a single word: "Nuts."

Bombs fell all Christmas day and night, but the following day the Fourth Armored Division of General George Patton arrived–the reinforcements the Allied troops had been hoping for all along.

Within a month, the battle was over and the march to Berlin began. It was the beginning of the end.

The Bible describes life as full of battles, and that is one reason we need Sabbath. We need the bombing to stop. We need reinforcements to arrive.

When Hebrews 4 says that God has fulfilled "Sabbath rest," it is referring to what He accomplished through Christ, who is called the great High Priest later in that chapter. Because He came, everything is different.

It is not by accident that one of the most-quoted sayings of Jesus is, "Come to me, all you who are weary and burdened, and I will give you rest. Take my yoke upon you and learn from me, for I am gentle and humble in heart, and you will find rest for your souls. For my yoke is easy and my burden is light" (Matthew 11:28-30). Who has not read those words and felt the tension inside loosen a bit? You read it, and then you read it again because you know this is what you need. You know it is right.

On the very first Christmas, the reinforcements arrived.

Make It Real: Take a piece of paper and write down Jesus' words, "Come to me, all you who are weary and burdened, and I will give you rest." List five times in your life when you were weary and burdened. Then complete this sentence: "Lord Jesus, the next time a burdensome time of my life comes, please be my reinforcement by . . ."

Day 7

The Lord said [to Elijah], "Go out and stand on the mountain in the presence of the Lord, for the Lord is about to pass by." Then a great and powerful wind tore the mountains apart and shattered the rocks before the Lord, but the Lord was not in the wind. After the wind there was an earthquake, but the Lord was not in the earthquake. After the earthquake came a fire, but the Lord was not in the fire. And after the fire came a gentle whisper.

1 KINGS 19:11-12

A research psychologist named Dr. John Calhoun did an experiment with mice in the 1970s in order to find out what would happen in overcrowded conditions. Eight mice were introduced into a comfortable, two-level, nine-foot-square cage. Before long (mice being what they are), the population grew to 160. The behavior of the mice stayed consistent. Over the next two years, however, as the population grew eventually to a staggering 2,200 mice in the same cage, behaviors began to change.

Dr. Calhoun kept the living conditions the same: There was always plenty of water and food. The temperature was ideal. There were no diseases. The only thing the mice lost was their privacy. There was no space and no opportunity to be alone.

The female mice began to wander around aimlessly. The males gathered in large clusters. Younger mice didn't fit in anywhere and occupied themselves with eating and sleeping. The mice grew increasingly apathetic. Their energy declined. Aggression set in. They attacked each other. They lost interest in reproduction. Then something happened—the population began to crash. Eventually, every mouse died, leaving no new generation.[1]

Now of course, mice are mice and people are people. But even if you take this experiment as a parable or metaphor, the result is chilling. God made us to live together with other people—we are designed to vitally connect in relationships with others. But we are also designed for solitary time, because some important things happen between us and God only when we are alone.

Henri Nouwen wrote, "To bring some solitude into our lives is one of the most necessary but also most difficult disciplines. Even though we may have a deep desire for solitude, we also experience a certain apprehension as we approach that solitary place and time. As soon as we are alone, without people to talk with, books to read, TV to watch, or phone calls to make, an inner chaos opens up to us."[2]

If you remove yourself from your normal attachments and discover in the solitude that your inner life is full of chaos, what do you do then? You ask God to do what He did in Genesis 1 when He took the void and the chaos and began to create a new world. You release to God any chaotic attitude you find in yourself (selfishness, greed, fear) and ask Him for the assurance that you will be okay when you let go. You ask God to give you one holy truth to focus on for that day—one thought that goes against the culture, that challenges your soul. And you ask Him to help you set a new Sabbath principle in your life.

Make It Real: Take half an hour sometime today when you happen to be alone and leave the TV, radio or any other soundmaker off. Ask God for the gift of His whisper. As you sense His presence, brainstorm some ideas for creating a personal time of Jubilee within the next six months.

Notes

1. J. R. Vallentyne, *Tragedy in Mouse Utopia* (Victoria, BC, Canada: Trafford Publishing, 2006).
2. Henri Nouwen, *Making All Things New* (New York: HarperOne, 1981), n.p.

WEEK 1

GROUP DISCUSSION QUESTIONS

1. Do you come from a background or family in which there was any idea or practice of Sabbath?

2. When you think about "rehearsing the truth that God and God alone is in control," does it strike you as a good proposition, or does it seem threatening or disturbing?

3. What areas of your life do you need to give God control of?

4. Do you think that the weekly pattern of your life has the appropriate variety of work and rest, public and private, or do you think you need to set a better pattern?

5. In what ways would you like prayer, reading Scripture, worship and contemplation to be stronger aspects of your life?

6. Why do you think it is difficult for us to cease what we normally do and do something different?

7. In what ways does worship help you to reorient your life, and what could you do so that worship has a deeper impact on you?

8. How do you react to Jesus' words, "Come to me, all you who are weary and burdened, and I will give you rest. Take my yoke upon you and learn from me, for I am gentle and humble in heart, and you will find rest for your souls" (Matthew 11:28-29)?

WEEK 2

REDEMPTION

Being Freed by God's Great Acts of Deliverance

Most of us at some time reach a point when we stop and wonder who or what is really in control of our lives.

Sometimes we stop in our tracks because we sense God is calling the question. We hear the distant sound of a trumpet blast (or maybe it's right in our ear). We know it demands an answer, and a good one. *Who is in control of my life?*

Sometimes it may be an uncomfortable or even desperate reality that prompts us to ask the question. Do any of these thoughts hit close to home?

1. Why do I feel as if other people are controlling my life, that I'm living to please other people and make them like me?

2. I know my boss is a jerk, but why can't I stop thinking about him and hearing his voice in my head 24 hours a day?

3. How did I get to the point that I obsessively overeat in order to feel calm?

4. Why am I so afraid of getting sick?

5. Why do I let my kids walk all over me?

6. I never in a million years would have thought I'd get into an extra-marital affair—how did I get here?

7. I wonder if I can get off cocaine before anybody suspects I'm using—or do they know already?

8. Why can't I stop looking at porn on my computer?

9. My wife insists that we move into yet another bigger house, but I know that our income isn't going to increase forever—how did we get on this treadmill?

10. I've blown my temper again at the kids, and now I feel awful—is this the way I'm going to always treat them?

Any of us could add a dozen different scenarios to this list. Life is often like walking through a thicket of bushes and thorns. Jesus warned us about the thorns and thistles that can choke out our spiritual life, the things that grab us and entangle us. And then, the more we struggle, the deeper the thorns set into us. We're trapped. We can't get out on our own. Someone needs to come and cut us out.

There are thorns and thistles in our heart attitudes. We are trapped when we succumb to temptations we never thought we would, or when we become obsessed with a person we want on our side, or when we get addicted to a substance or damaging habit. If we're continually distracted in life by the material things we do not have but long for, or by the material things we have that demand our servicing and attention, then we are trapped, even though we may fool ourselves into believing we are in control.

Redemption is what we need.

What Is Redemption?

Redemption is God's mighty act of delivering us from anyone or anything that holds us in bondage. It is God's way of getting our lives back.

We use the word more simply when we talk about someone "redeeming" his reputation or "redeeming" a pledge. If a football team performs poorly one weekend and then spectacularly the following Sunday, the sports reporter may say, "They really redeemed themselves today."

We call some select novels and films "stories of redemption" when the plot turns on someone regaining his or her life: a falsely accused person in prison goes free; a selfish, hopeless person does something heroic; a forgotten group of people are rescued. The permutations are endless, but the underlying dynamic in all stories of redemption is getting away from some dominating force and breaking into freedom.

We know things are bad in someone's life when others say that he or she is "beyond redemption." What a horrifying thought, that any of us are so guilty, so much in bondage or so twisted that there is no hope anymore. That is something the Scriptures never say. No one is ever beyond redemption—unless, of course, he or she pursues a course of life that is intentionally in bondage.

All of us have something about our lives that we would like to redeem. To get back our reputation. To rebuild something that has been torn down. To get out from under the control of our own faults and limitations or the oppression of someone else. We can't change the past, but God redeems our present and our future.

The landmark historical event signaling that things can be different—that redemption is real, that we can get our lives back again—is the Exodus. When hundreds of thousands of Hebrews who were held in cruel servitude by Egypt's pharaoh heard the following word from God, they knew that things could be different . . . but only if a Redeemer God made it so:

> I am the LORD, and I will bring you out from under the yoke of the Egyptians. I will free you from being slaves to them, and I will redeem you with an outstretched arm and with mighty acts of judgment. I will take you as my own people, and I will be your God. Then you will know that I am the LORD your God, who brought you out from under the yoke of the Egyptians (Exodus 6:6-7).

We agonize over how overlords like the hard-hearted Egyptian pharaoh rise up in the first place, and why God doesn't intervene sooner. We must, of course, consider the fact that human beings are created with the ability to choose extraordinarily good paths and the ability to choose monstrous deeds instead, but no answer to the question will ever mask the pain people endure. Sometimes we can console ourselves with the knowledge that all despots fall eventually. Their lives are like a horrible song sung once, and then the next generation takes its turn, deciding whether to sing a similar song or to strike a different note. Often it is when people see that they are beginning to repeat the patterns of those who have gone before that they stop in their tracks, take a look around, turn to God in fear and start backing away from the cliff. I have known many people who grew up in alcoholic homes who were told that it was highly likely that they would continue the sick legacy of their father or mother. Yet they decided to leave a different legacy instead. It isn't always easy, but with God the Redeemer, it *is* possible.

Across the centuries, the marching of Hebrew men and women, boys and girls, out of slavery and into the clear but sometimes cloudy skies of freedom, has been the central captivating story and symbol of hope through redemption. The Exodus was God's way of saying not just that He stood against an evil pharaoh, a single despot who stole life from one nation, the Hebrews, but that He stands against all injustice and has promised judgment on every despot, including the ruler of an evil empire and the husband who beats his wife.

Redemption on the Day of Atonement

The Bible, taken as a whole, is one long story of redemption. Since the time when something went terribly awry in the human race, God has been offering ways for us to gain our lives back. And—as is widely recognized in most of the stories of redemption that we tell—gaining life very often comes through a sacrifice.

The holiest day in the Hebrew calendar falls on the tenth day of the month of Tishri. It is the conclusion of a 10-day period, the *Yamim Noraim*, the Days of Awe. (I love that phrase. It suggests that a holiday should be a *holy* day, and should prompt a sense of awe in our lives. What good is Christmas or Easter if they don't make us stand in awe of God's great sweeping movement in history?) The tenth day of the month of Tishri is *Yom Kippur*, the Day of Atonement, which is all about redemption. As stipulated in Leviticus 16, on that one day the high priest made a special sacrifice for the sins of all the people. On the Day of Atonement every year the people would know again that God had not forgotten them—that He would lead them out of bondage once again.

We can read details about the Day of Atonement ritual in Leviticus 23 and 25. The high priest stepped out in full view of spectators who had gathered. On this day, he wore only simple white linen—nothing bright, embroidered or jeweled. Two goats were brought to him, one of which was sacrificed and its blood brought into the Most Holy Place of the Tabernacle (in later generations, the Temple). Some of the blood was sprinkled on the cover of the Ark of the Covenant, the so-called "mercy seat."

None of the people could see. They knew what was happening, but only the high priest was allowed into the Holy of Holies, and only on that one day. There was mystery here. The fact that only one man on only one day of the year could go into that inner chamber added to the sense of awe and holiness of this day.

Redemption remains mysterious to this day. Why does a sister offer her kidney to her brother? Why does a soldier throw himself on a grenade to save his buddies? Why do some young adults go off to conflict-ridden parts of the world to try to make a difference? Why do we want to hang on to hope for those who seem hopeless, who seem even "beyond redemption"? It's almost like we instinctively know that there are strong and sometimes overwhelming tides of destruction in life, but that there is also an opposite principle at work, a dynamic undercurrent of redemption. And people who did get their lives back will stand up and shout it to the world.

The other goat that was brought to the high priest on the Day of Atonement was taken to the edge of the wilderness, where people gathered to watch the drama that was about to unfold. The priest laid his hands on the goat's head, paused and then let the goat scurry away into the wilderness. The people watched. The goat wandered this way and that, and finally disappeared in the distance. The annual ritual of the scapegoat on the Day of Atonement was a riveting picture of the sins of the people being carried far, far away—so far that the guilt could never be seen again. So far away that the sin-infection was wiped out forever. It was the day of redemption.

Redemption and Jubilee

The Day of Atonement is an annual holiday, but Leviticus stipulates that every 49 years, the sound of the shofar on the Day of Atonement marks the beginning of a Year of Jubilee. The following verses in Leviticus 25 describe some of the redemption themes of the Year of Jubilee. They may seem a bit complicated or difficult to understand, but they are important:

> If one of your countrymen becomes poor and sells some of his property, his nearest relative is to come and redeem what his countryman has sold. If, however, a man has no one to redeem it for him but he himself prospers and acquires sufficient means to redeem it, he is to determine the value for the years since he sold it and refund the balance to the man to whom he sold it; he can then go back to his own property. But if he does not acquire the means to repay him, what he sold will remain in the possession of the buyer until the Year of Jubilee. It will be returned in the Jubilee, and he can then go back to his property.
>
> If a man sells a house in a walled city, he retains the right of redemption a full year after its sale. During that time he may redeem it. If it is not redeemed before a full year has passed, the house in the walled city shall belong permanently to the buyer and his descendants. It is not to be returned in the Jubilee. But houses in villages without walls around them are to be considered as open country. They can be redeemed, and they are to be returned in the Jubilee.
>
> The Levites always have the right to redeem their houses in the Levitical towns, which they possess. So the property of the Levites is redeemable—that is, a house sold in any town they hold—and is to be returned in the Jubilee, because the houses in the towns of the Levites are their property among the Israelites (vv. 25-33).

The cultural details in this passage boil down to this: Once every 50 years (basically, once in a lifetime) the Israelites were to square everything up, to bring people back to a livable situation, to be redeemed, to gain their lives back. Specifically, this meant that land was to be returned to its original family. In the push and pull of war and famine and servitude, this was a way to make sure that people didn't get displaced from or dispossessed of the family homestead. Many people were forced to give up control of their land by leasing it to others. Jubilee was a way of saying that the lease was fulfilled; it was time to get back what was originally theirs. Homesteads should go back to displaced families (this may be hard for us to understand in the modern world, when property is defined by contracts and deeds).

Now in some cases, a well-off relative helped out a family member who was under duress. This is the dynamic behind the story of Ruth and Boaz, recounted in the dramatic book of Ruth in the Old Testament. The well-to-do Boaz was the *goel*, the "kinsman-redeemer," who intervened so that a needy young woman, Ruth, would not be destitute. (Many people cannot even imagine a time when relatives assumed that they may be used by God to help someone in the family get his or her life back!)

Behind the fine points of Leviticus 25 is the larger principle that the earth is the Lord's and everything in it. Human beings don't really own land—God does. Yet we have a very hard time remembering that. Think about how many conflicts there have been over territory. For two years, the Ethiopians and Eritreans waged a bloody war over a stretch of rocky, barren land at the cost of tens of thousands of lives. Many wonder how the land of Iraq will be governed over the long term; Shi'ites, Sunnis and Kurds continue to violently dispute control of the provinces. The Israeli-Palestinian conflict has been going on for over 60 years.

For an example more close to home, consider how difficult it was for the U.S. government to acknowledge that land should be given back to Native Americans, who lived here long before the first colonists arrived. When the government finally did, it offered small parcels called "reservations," which, many people argue (for good reason), do not come close to making restitution for what was stolen.

We have no historical records to tell us whether or not the children of Abraham faithfully carried out God's decrees of Jubilee, giving those in debt a new start and returning familial lands to those who were dispossessed. But we do know that Jubilee was an ambitious—even audacious—command. It demanded a settling of all scores, true social justice. It imposed a law higher than those defined by contracts and deeds.

Redemption is a radical idea. Imagine what would happen if God told you that the house you bought at basement bargain price on a mortgage foreclosure had to be turned over to the original owners because they lost the house in distressing circumstances. Given the complexities of life today, it is hard to fathom, but it was written into the Hebrews' law. They knew that God wanted redemption. He wanted people to get their lives back, even if it meant others giving up their profit or position.

Maybe redemption doesn't have to be so rare. I've met people who have given their spouse another chance to be faithful in the marriage—not because they are legally bound to, but because they believe that unfaithfulness can become a thing of the past. I know people who have offered their teenage children another chance even after terrible choices have been made. I have met people who have forgiven a debt when it looked like there was an opportunity for the indebted person to start over with a clean slate. And I know many people who have forgiven people who wronged them terribly, and thereby freed them to begin the relationship again. Forgive people and you free them—not because you are a tolerant or permissive person, but because you believe that God wants people to have the opportunity to start again.

The Deep History of Redemption

The first time I met the pediatrician who would be my children's doctor was when he visited the hospital room where my wife was holding our firstborn. It was the morning after our new baby had arrived; she wasn't even 24 hours old yet. I remember being surprised at my apprehension as the doctor took our baby, checking the movement of every limb, placing a big black stethoscope against her pink skin, poking and scoping with lighted instruments. It was like a rite of passage.

I try to imagine what it was like for first-time parents Mary and Joseph as they brought their newborn son all the way to Jerusalem, up the steps of the great Temple, to dedicate their firstborn just as the descendants of Abraham had been doing for millennia. They knew that the offering of one's firstborn to God was a reminder of the Exodus, when the firstborn children of the Israelites were spared the plague that descended on the Egyptians. When people like Joseph and Mary brought a couple of doves or pigeons to offer as a sacrifice, they knew they were hearkening back to the deep history of redemption. Exodus 13:11-13 says that the Israelites were to "give over" to the Lord the first offspring of every womb. That meant a literal sacrifice of the firstborn among the livestock, but firstborn children could be redeemed by an alternative sacrifice.

And so Mary and Joseph approached the Temple, having purchased a couple of birds for a sacrifice that would symbolize the redemption of their son. They were redeeming the Redeemer. Three decades later, not far from the Temple mount, their son would be crucified. That was the day of redemption. In the death of the Son of God, we gained back our lives.

God had set up a way for people who had fallen into a hole, who were dispossessed and entrapped, to find a way out. But getting the family homestead back in the Old Covenant era was just a foreshadowing of what God planned to do in Jesus the Redeemer, who came to get the whole of our lives back. Getting back the home your great-grandparents intended you to have is a great thing, but gaining a place in the household of God–particularly when you feel like you have no spiritual home–is incredible! Getting out of bonded servitude is indeed a great thing, but getting out of the spiritual bondage of bitterness, despair or injustice is freedom that can never be taken away, even into eternity.

The deep foundation, the long history of redemption, had been laid. The Exodus out of slavery in Egypt, the annual rituals of the Day of Atonement, the blowing of the trumpet every 50 years to inaugurate the Year of Jubilee–these powerful, liberating events pointed to the ultimate redemption God had planned for the human race.

One day when Jesus' disciples were begging Him for a special place in His kingdom, Jesus silenced them with a statement about why He came: "The Son of Man did not come to be served, but to serve, and to give his life as a ransom for many" (Mark 10:45). Throughout the Old Testament, God had pointed to Himself as the great Redeemer. Now Jesus was saying, "*I* will redeem you; *I* will be the ransom price."

Long before any moviemaker or novelist had a hero declare "Take me instead of her," Jesus said it, and He said it with His life. In Acts 20:28, the apostle Paul tells church leaders that beyond all the expectations and agendas in the Church and in society, they are called to "shepherd the church of God which he bought with his own blood." *Bought* . . . that's the central idea. The God who owns the universe bought back people whose lives are controlled by someone or something else. He tells us today, "You are precious to Me. You have all kinds of enemies without and within, but I went to the cross in order to redeem you, to purchase you back. I hold the deed to your life . . . and that means you are free."

Redeemed for What?

Christ redeemed us *from* sin and *for* purity. Colossians 1:14 says that in Christ we have redemption, the forgiveness of sins, while Ephesians 1 says:

> [God] chose us in him before the creation of the world to be holy and blameless in his sight. In love he predestined us to be adopted as his sons through Jesus Christ, in accordance with his pleasure and will—to the praise of his glorious grace, which he has freely given us in the

One he loves. In him we have redemption through his blood, the forgiveness of sins, in accordance with the riches of God's grace that he lavished on us with all wisdom and understanding (vv. 4-8).

And Titus 2 says that Christ "gave himself for us to redeem us from all wickedness and to purify for himself a people that are his very own, eager to do what is good" (v. 14). Is that who we want to be? People liberated from our own wicked thoughts, purified, owned by God and eager to do what is good?

Who is in control of my life? That is the central question to which redemption is the answer: God has redeemed us from whatever and whomever has kept us in slavery, controlling us and limiting our freedom. But how, practically speaking, can we ensure that we never fall into bondage again?

1. Realize You Do Not Have to Live Under the Mastery of Sin

You and I will never be sinless in this life, but that does not mean that we must give in to the mastery of sin. Sometimes sin is a stumbling; other times, it is an intentional walk away from the life of freedom. A lonely woman has a liaison with a married man (she stumbles), but then she meets with him again and again and again. It becomes a full-fledged affair. She tries to step out of it, but she keeps going back. She is mastered by her desires. She is "owned" by adultery. She is "walking in sin." The one way that she can get her life back is not by trying to wrestle control back to herself, but by placing herself under the ownership of God and allowing Him to redeem her from the slavery of infidelity.

2. Don't Let Any Other Person Be Your God

You and I can obey and serve the one true God or we can choose substitutes. This usually means other people. A god can be anyone who exercises control, who demands service, who wields great power or who asks for adoration.

Our family has a dog that is basically obsessed with us. She watches our every move, follows us from one room to the next and could not be more pleased than when we give her a command. Don't be like the family dog. We squander our dignity when we allow another person to be the object of our obsession, when we make a human being god in our lives, when we think we will find a place in life if we worship another person. Because Christ redeemed us, we can live free from any attempts others may make to have a despotic rule in our lives. We are already owned—by God! No cult can make a claim on us. No spouse or brother or sister can define who we are. No one can make an arbitrary "call" on our lives and impose it. We are called by one God, the God who bought us back.

3. Let Go of Legalism

Given human nature, we always drift toward legalism (the "way of the code," see Romans 7:6; Colossians 2:14) or toward making up our own standards of righteousness. We like it that way. We are in control. We set the rules. We decide when we've done something of eternal significance. We tell God when we are acceptable (and let Him know about all the unacceptable people around who He should *really* be worried about). Legalism is kindergarten spirituality. It defines righteousness as "don't do these three things, and make sure you do these three."

Legalism kills the spirit and arouses pride. It just doesn't work. Turning spiritual disciplines into boxes that need checking off doesn't work. Coming up with measurable goals for spiritual growth doesn't work. Perfectionism in Christian relationships doesn't work. We must trust the God of redemption to lead us into the full freedom of becoming mature sons and daughters of God.

4. Learn that "You Have Been Bought at a Price"

Accept your body as not your own, but as God's temple. We are concerned about health in our society, which is a good thing—not just so that we live longer, but because our bodies are temples of the Holy Spirit. And they should be treated as such! A believer doesn't "sleep around," because the temple of God is dedicated only to Him. Everything in life changes when we really believe that we are temples of God's Spirit. And it's not just that your body has been "bought with a price"—*you* have been bought. Your mind is owned by God, and He expects you to fill it with noble thoughts through your conversations, your reading and your prayer. Your heart is owned by God—that place where your motives come from, where your values are shaped, where bias can creep in; how are you letting God take ownership? Everything is different when we believe that we are not our own. What could have made us think that in the first place?

5. Seek Intervention If You Are Subject to Obsession or Addiction

Our society has produced an array of obsessions and addictions, such as gambling, substance abuse, pornography . . . the list goes on and on. One thing that is true of every obsession or addiction: It is all a matter of control. A person starts down a path and then becomes controlled by the thing. The only solution is to gain back control. But here is the two-sided truth of the matter: "self-control" is a "fruit of the Spirit" (see Galatians 5:23). In other words, we can control ourselves only insofar as God controls us. Getting help to learn how to give God control is an important first step toward freedom.

6. Seek Counsel and Correction

If others have consistently told you that you are unduly carried away with anything (rage, resentment, work, leisure, food, sex, possessions), seek wise counsel and correction. We can be "owned" by an impulse or vice within us. Now, we are likely to resist someone else telling us that we have a problem; none of us likes to admit that we are out of control. But the wise person who hears that kind of warning on numerous occasions and from numerous sources stops in his or her tracks, makes an honest self-assessment and asks God for His help to get back under His control, and His control alone.

The Lion of Judah

I found a remarkable story reported by the Associated Press that many may find hard to believe—but the facts were corroborated by more than one source. The striking headline is "Lions Rescue, Guard Beaten Ethiopian Girl." It reads:

> A 12-year-old girl who was abducted and beaten by men trying to force her into a marriage was found being

guarded by three lions who apparently had chased off her captors, a policeman said Tuesday. The girl, missing for a week, had been taken by seven men who wanted to force her to marry one of them, said Sgt. Wondimu Wedajo, speaking by telephone from the provincial capital of Bita Genet, about 350 miles southwest of Addis Ababa. She was beaten repeatedly before she was found June 9 by police and relatives on the outskirts of Bita Genet, Wondimu said. She had been guarded by the lions for about half a day, he said. "They stood guard until we found her and then they just left her like a gift and went back into the forest," Wondimu said. "If the lions had not come to her rescue, then it could have been much worse. Often these young girls are raped and severely beaten to force them to accept the marriage," he said. Tilahun Kassa, a local government official who corroborated Wondimu's version of the events, said one of the men had wanted to marry the girl against her wishes. "Everyone thinks this is some kind of miracle, because normally the lions would attack people," Wondimu said. Stuart Williams, a wildlife expert with the rural development ministry, said the girl may have survived because she was crying from the trauma of her attack. "A young girl whimpering could be mistaken for the mewing sound from a lion cub, which in turn could explain why they didn't eat her," Williams said. Ethiopia's lions, famous for their large black manes, are the country's national symbol and adorn statues and the local currency.[1]

There are few greater symbols of power in the animal kingdom than the lion. The tribe of Judah, the tribe from which Jesus descended, is represented by the lion. The book of Revelation describes the ultimate victory of Christ over everyone and everything that would try to "own" us:

> Then one of the elders said to me, "Do not weep! See, the Lion of the tribe of Judah, the Root of David, has triumphed. He is able to open the scroll and its seven seals" (5:5).

I believe one reason we don't live in the light of redemption is that we don't have the confidence that it is true. We want to be released from what enslaves us, whether it's a bad habit, a cyclical sin, a destructive relationship or a faulty way of thinking. But can we be released? Really? Is "redeemer" just a word we use for Jesus, or can He actually free us today?

Dare to trust that the Lion of Judah is mighty enough to defeat anything or anyone holding us in bondage.

Note

1. Anthony Mitchell, "Lions Rescue, Guard Beaten Girl," AP via Persian Journal Online, June 22, 2005. http://www.iranian.ws/cgi-bin/iran_news/exec/view.cgi/13/7733 (accessed April 2008).

DAILY REFLECTIONS

Day 8

I am the LORD, and I will bring you out from under the yoke of the Egyptians. I will free you from being slaves to them, and I will redeem you with an outstretched arm and with mighty acts of judgment.

EXODUS 6:6

Redemption. Let that word turn around and around in your mind this week. Redemption means to be freed by someone able to purchase your freedom. This is what God has done for us. He goes far beyond a simple declaration of freedom and *makes it happen*. If you need freedom from guilt, from shame, from an obsession, from addiction—whatever you need freedom from—God has made it a reality by buying you out of that bondage.

Picture yourself back in the Deep South at the turn of the nineteenth century, when many a slave stood on an auction block hearing bids cast about, determining who would be his or her next owner. Imagine standing in humiliation and degradation. Being evaluated on how strong your muscles are and how much toil someone can get out of you.

Now imagine a mysterious bidder at the back of the crowd who keeps raising the price. You get the sense that this buyer will not be outbid, that there is no price too high for him to back down. In a battle of wills, a malevolent and resentful bidder (an evil master doing his best to snatch you away to continue the abuse and humiliation) only causes the good Man at the back to offer more and more. And the good Man wins. He has more resources than anyone can match.

And then your new Owner does this remarkable thing: He takes you into His household not as a slave, but as a son or daughter. He provides your food, clothing, shelter, and even makes you a legal heir to all of His riches.

This is what the Bible says about God the Redeemer. His name is Lord Almighty and what He does is redeem. We are freed by Someone who is able to purchase our freedom. "Our Redeemer—the LORD Almighty is his name—is the Holy One of Israel" (Isaiah 47:4).

There is a Redeemer, Jesus, God's own Son,
Precious Lamb of God, Messiah, Holy One.
Thank you, O my Father, for giving us Your Son
And leaving Your Spirit, 'til Your work on earth is done.[1]

This week as we explore the Jubilee theme of redemption, count your blessings—literally. Recognize that Christ has bought you at a price and be grateful. Decide to submit to His Lordship in every area of your life.

Make the first words out of your mouth every morning: "Thank You, Lord, for another day. I belong to You. Help me to be aware of my identity in You in every part of my life today." In everything give praise: "He lifted me out of the slimy pit, out of the mud and mire; he set my feet on a rock and gave me a firm place to stand" (Psalm 40:2). Thank God that He has adopted you into His family.

Make It Real: On a piece of paper, list two things that God has freed you from. These could be past shame, an addiction, an oppressive relationship or something else. Pray out loud, "Thank You, Lord, for freeing me from . . ." Cross out the two things and place the paper where you will see it regularly as a reminder that you are no longer bound.

Day 9

Joseph and Mary took Jesus to Jerusalem to present him to the LORD (as it is written in the Law of the LORD, "Every firstborn male is to be consecrated to the LORD").

LUKE 2:22-23

It took a lot of effort for Mary and Joseph to take their newborn son all the way to Jerusalem to fulfill their obligation to consecrate Him according to the Law of Moses. The rocky, dusty roads were well-worn from the frequent traffic of people and animals from Bethlehem to Jerusalem. Up and down white rocky hills and then, over the last crest, the edge of the city came into view and the spectacular sight of the Temple, majestic and stately. They may have come over the hill and down the Mount of Olives where Jesus, three decades later, would enter the city for the last time in His short life.

How glad they were that God did not require the sacrifice of their son, but provided a way of redemption. On this day, their sacrifice was a pair of doves or pigeons.

The courtyard around the Temple would have been bustling with people coming and going, doing their business. An ordinary man and woman with their baby would not have been noticed. But an old man named Simeon, who knew God's salvation was just around the corner, had a supernatural message from Him that this baby, in those parents' arms, was the One who was to come. Taking Jesus in his own arms, Simeon said, "My eyes have seen your salvation, which you have prepared in the sight of all people, a light for revelation to the Gentiles and for glory to your people Israel" (Luke 2:30-32).

With the sacrifice offered, Mary and Joseph left Jerusalem, relieved that their firstborn son was redeemed—not knowing that He would become the true Redemption, the true sacrifice, for them and for everyone else.

What about us? When we consider Jesus, are we able to say, "My eyes have seen Your salvation"? We are not just looking at the infant Jesus as Simeon was. We see Christ in the fullness of His life and with centuries of His influence. Redemption is not a theory. Redemption came, in the flesh.

Make It Real: Think of a time when someone sacrificed for you—maybe a parent, a teacher or a friend. Take some time today to let that person know that you appreciate the sacrifice they made for you. In the same way, give thanks to God for His ultimate sacrifice in giving us His Son.

Day 10

We wait for the blessed hope—the glorious appearing of our great God and Savior, Jesus Christ, who gave himself for us to redeem us from all wickedness and to purify for himself a people that are his very own, eager to do what is good.

TITUS 2:13-14

At the height of his singing career, Johnny Cash was one of the most recognizable faces and voices in the world. But Cash became an out-of-control drug addict and loathed himself for it. He decided to end it all.

He went to a place near the Tennessee River called Nickajack Cave. He crawled, walked and shimmied deeper and deeper into the labyrinth, determined to go on until his flashlight died—which it did. Later Cash wrote, "I was as far from God as I have ever been. My separation from him, the deepest and most ravaging of the various kinds of loneliness I'd ever felt over the years, seemed complete."[2]

But then something happened in him. With a sense of utter peace and sobriety, Cash realized that he was not in charge of his own destiny. He turned around and began to crawl in the direction he had come from. Hours later, feeling a breeze and seeing light, he realized God had saved him from that grave. As he emerged into the light of day where he had abandoned his Jeep, his mother and a close friend were waiting. He had told neither of them where he would be that day.

In Christ, God has made redemption possible. It is never too late for us. We are never too far gone. God is never too far away. As Titus 2 says, Christ was given to redeem us from all wickedness and to purify us. Johnny Cash knew that someone greater than he needed to break him free. Somebody stronger needed to supply the price to set him free. Many people do not hit rock bottom the way Cash did and do not have a sense of the nearness of wickedness or the need for purification. But the cave starts getting dark just a few steps in. Now is the time—every day is the time—to accept by faith the redemption from wickedness and the purifying power of Christ.

Make It Real: Sometime today, take a few minutes to pray and think in a very dark room (the darker the better). Tell God where you need the light of His truth and purity in your life and also how you need guidance. Think about the future "glorious appearing of our great God and Savior, Jesus Christ" (Titus 2:13).

Day 11

If one of your countrymen becomes poor and sells some of his property, his nearest relative is to come and redeem what his countryman has sold . . . It will be returned in the Year of Jubilee, and he can then go back to his property.

LEVITICUS 25:25,28

Consumer debt is at an all-time high today. Skillful marketers have developed remarkable ways to convince people that they need all kinds of things and that they deserve them *now*. Buy now, pay later. And then, boy do you pay!

This kind of indebtedness can quickly become one kind of bondage. Someone else has a claim on you. The rate of interest is a set of chains that holds you. It would be wonderful if someone could come and just break the chains, forgive the debt and let you start over.

In the dry, unpredictable and sometimes unfruitful land of Israel, it was very easy for people to fall short on resources, to go into deep debt and to lose their house or land. The way others acquired that property was frequently illegal, unethical and unjust.

God determined that in the Year of Jubilee, people would have a second chance. Property long owned by families that had been snatched away would be redeemed. In this buy-back plan (done only once every 50 years, mind you), God stipulated that people should be able to return to their ancestral property. If relatives can buy back the land, they should buy it. If partial payment can be made, they should start now. One way or another, there should be a return to the way things used to be.

Does the principle of forgiving debt from the Old Testament have any relevance today? A lot of people would like credit card companies to forgive their debt and let them go. Or they would like to turn back the hands of time and make far different decisions about their indebtedness.

There is a place for the forgiveness of debt. All of us will have an opportunity some day to help someone out of a jam or to release someone from an obligation to us. We may worry that if we bail someone out, he or she won't learn from his or her experience. But sometimes the risk is worth it.

Make It Real: Think of someone who could use your help today. Pray for that person and ask for guidance about how you could help them. Maybe he or she is having trouble paying rent this month or maybe he or she is just getting behind on taking care of the lawn. Think of a way to give someone else a break today!

Day 12

Christ redeemed us from the curse of the law by becoming a curse for us, for it is written: "Cursed is everyone who is hung on a tree." He redeemed us in order that the blessing given to Abraham might come to the Gentiles through Christ Jesus, so that by faith we might receive the promise of the Spirit.

GALATIANS 3:13-14

It may come as a surprise that, of all the things God has freed us from, He has also freed us from "the curse of the law." *But didn't God Himself give the Law on Mount Sinai through Moses? Don't we need a Law from God in order to define right and wrong and to keep us on track in life?*

When parents raise their kids in order to instill a spiritual and moral compass, they have to keep things simple and concrete early on: "Don't touch this. Don't go there. Don't steal your brother's toys. Do obey." When adolescence comes, parents try to help their kids develop an understanding about *why* they should do this and not that. And then there is that stage when a parent says, "I've taught you as much as I can. You're an adult now, and you'll be making all your own decisions. You're no longer under the rules of the house. You have to build your own home and family."

That, in part, is what redemption from the Law means. (Paul calls this redemption "dying to the law.") God says, "It's time to grow up!" And not because we are more morally capable today than the people of God in the Old Testament, but because this dramatic thing has happened: God's Son has come. He is our redemption—our liberator. He is the Jubilee. Blow the trumpet loudly!

But Christ has also liberated us from "the curse of the law," the indictment on our heads resulted from comparing God's righteous standards to the reality of our lives. One of the greatest manifestos of freedom ever written is Paul's epistle to the Galatians. Freedom, freedom, freedom is the theme that runs throughout the letter. Galatians 3:13 says that "Christ redeemed us from the curse of the law by becoming a curse for us, for it is written, 'Cursed is everyone who is hung on a tree.' "

Paul quotes Deuteronomy 21:23 here, and takes that verse as an allusion to Christ being hung on the cross. Jesus' sacrifice was a premeditated, pre-planned act of God. He knew that the human race was going to need rescue, so "when the time had fully come, God sent his son, born of a woman, born under law, to redeem those under law, that we might receive the full rights of sons" (Galatians 4:4).

The moral law of the Old Testament, including the Ten Commandments, tested us and we came up short. But Jesus Christ came and made the sacrifice, fulfilling the saying, "Cursed is everyone who is hung on a tree."

Make It Real: Think of one area of your life in which it's time to grow above the rules and do something because it's right rather than because you have to. For example, think about what you can do today to be a responsible driver. Be a responsible driver not just to avoid a ticket, but because it's the right thing to do.

Day 13

After the LORD brings you into the land of the Canaanites and gives it to you, as he promised on oath to you and your forefathers, you are to give over to the LORD the first offspring of every womb. All the firstborn males of your livestock belong to the LORD. Redeem with a lamb every firstborn donkey, but if you do not redeem it, break its neck. Redeem every firstborn among your sons.

EXODUS 13:11-13

If you've ever walked through Arlington National Cemetery in Washington, DC, you probably stopped and stared at the sight of thousands of pure white crosses spread across the grassy knolls so solemn, peaceful and orderly. But when you let yourself think of what those crosses represent—one for every human life sacrificed in war—it really sinks in: Each one stands for somebody's next-door neighbor, somebody's buddy, somebody's son. In Arlington, the uniformity of the crosses reminds us that though individual identity is important, more important still is the act of sacrifice.

When the Israelites heard the word "redemption," they always thought back to that great act of liberation, when God took all of His people out from under the oppressive hand of Pharaoh. On the night of the Exodus when the firstborn of Egypt died, the firstborn son in each Israelite household was redeemed with a Passover lamb.

As God took the people toward a new land, He stipulated that they should sacrifice to Him the very first of everything they had and did: the first sheaves of grain harvested from the field, the firstborn of the cattle, the firstborn child. But wait a minute! Jehovah was not the kind of God who asked for human sacrifice as a sign of commitment to Him. No, God instead said to the people, "Consider your firstborn sacrificed to Me (to keep in mind that you should offer Me the very first of what you have and do), but I will let you buy back the life of your firstborn child. I will let you redeem your child." For generations, God's people "offered" their firstborn children, but received them back through sacrifice.

At the end of the film *Saving Private Ryan*, a dying captain sits slumped against a stone wall and tells a lieutenant with his last breath, "Earn this." Like that young lieutenant, we will never be able to earn our redemption . . . but we can live up to it.

Make It Real: Practice sacrifice today by letting others go before you. Serve your family dinner before taking your portion, or let someone get in front of you in line at the bank or at the grocery store.

Day 14

At that time they will see the Son of Man coming in a cloud with power and great glory. When these things begin to take place, stand up and lift up your heads, because your redemption is drawing near.

LUKE 21:27-28

Do you worry about the end of the world and think about what will happen then? What do you think will happen to you?

Of course, a lot of people don't think much about it, assuming that they'll be dead and gone long before any apocalyptic events unfold. Or, as a character in an American comic strip said: "Don't worry about the world coming to an end today. It's already tomorrow in Australia."

Everybody wonders about the end of the world in one way or another. Scientists predict the sun will run low on energy, become unstable and expand into a red giant that will engulf Earth. (Don't worry about that happening soon, though. The sun is going to be fine for another 5 billion years.) Other scientists warn that a massive asteroid could collide into Earth at almost any time—and they can't track such objects until the last minute. And since the advent of nuclear weapons, people have worried about humanity unleashing man-made demons and engulfing the planet in deadly radioactivity.

When Jesus' followers asked Him about the end, He said that wars and revolutions would come and go. Kingdom would rise against kingdom. There would be earthquakes, famines and pestilences. And persecution.

But the end of the world as we know it will not be an accidental cataclysm; it will be the intentional act of God drawing this history to an end and beginning a new era with a New Creation. The Son of God will come with "power and great glory"—and that is when final redemption draws near. Remember that *redemption* means to be freed by someone who is able to purchase your freedom. On the final day, the world will see Jesus Christ, the Redeemer, free His people from one world and release them in glory into another.

Make It Real: Throughout today, do this exercise: When you see something good or beautiful (a part of God's creation, a person you appreciate, a good conversation), say to yourself, "Better than this." Use this phrase to remind yourself that the New Creation will be better than the very best we experience in this life.

Notes

1. © Melody Green, "There Is a Redeemer," Ears to Hear Music, Oceanside, CA.
2. Johnny Cash, *Cash: The Autobiography* (New York: HarperCollins, 1997), pp. 170-171.

WEEK 2

GROUP DISCUSSION QUESTIONS

1. Redemption is the promise that God can and does free us from people or things that would control us. Can you think of someone who is trying to control you in some unhealthy way?

2. What are some of the bad habits, obsessions or addictions that can exercise control over a person's life? Is there someone you know whom you are concerned about?

3. What are some reasons we want to believe that we control life? Why do we have a hard time giving control into the hands of God?

4. What is a "story of redemption" that is memorable to you? (It might be a book, a movie or a story that focuses on someone being wonderfully freed.) Why?

5. Who is someone you know who has experienced redemption in his or her life? How?

6. How does accepting the truth that "you have been bought at a price" make a difference in your life?

7. How have you seen legalism (measuring spiritual strength by how much we control) kill the spirit?

8. How does believing that Jesus really has redeemed us make a difference in your life today?

WEEK 3

FREEDOM

Cherishing the Liberty that God Brings to Every Area of Life

In the movie *The Shawshank Redemption*, three very different men get out of a horrendous prison run by a corrupt warden and wicked guards. One of them, a man wrongly accused of murder, gets free by breaking out. Year after year, he chisels through the plaster and rock of his cell wall, hiding the chips in his pants leg and depositing them into the yard, until one night, he makes his way through a sewage pipe more than 500 yards before falling into a river. It is a stormy night, and he holds his hands toward the skies as the cleansing rain washes him of the grime and the shame.

A second man, the escapee's best friend and a model prisoner, endures year after year of denied parole until the board finally believes that he has been reformed. They stamp his file "PAROLED" and, as a free but somewhat lost man, he makes his way to his friend (who is, by this time, living on a beautiful coast in Mexico).

The third man, a sweet old gentleman whose whole world has become the prison and the small library he maintains, is released from prison after serving half a century. To him, the outside world is frightening and unknown. Freedom gives him a life of possibilities, but he doesn't know what to do with them. To him, freedom is oppressive, and so he stands on a chair in his apartment and puts a noose around his neck.

You and I cherish freedom. We go to war to defend it. Some even lay down their lives so that others may be free.

At the same time, we don't always know what to do with freedom. Slaves were freed by the Emancipation Proclamation, but those who found their way to free states did not necessarily find a free life; we're still getting over slavery. The world was gratified to see the ink-marked thumbs of people on the first election day in Iraq, but building a genuinely free society requires more than one election. Freedom takes generations to become reality.

And then there are the personal stories of gaining freedom only to find that living freely is harder than was believed. The woman who finally gets that divorce she has been wanting for years, but who somehow ends up feeling not free at all. The man who is liberated from his addiction to cocaine, but then has to answer the question, *What's next?* Cast one demon out, and there is a gang of others lying in wait to make their way in.

But it doesn't have to be that way.

In the last chapter we looked at the Jubilee theme of redemption, which is God's mighty act of delivering us from anybody or anything that would hold us in bondage. For that to happen, the Son of God gave His life. The result of redemption, of getting one's life back again, is *freedom*. Wondrous freedom. God-backed freedom.

On any given day, every one of us needs to be set free from something. It is not just the heroin addict or the alcoholic who needs God's dramatic liberating power. What some of us need on a daily basis is freedom from fear, whether it be from fear of death, fear of abandonment, fear of child abduction, fear of failure at work, or fear of cancer. Some need freedom from fear of God—not the good kind of fear that is awe-producing respect, but the pathological kind of fear that takes over when someone has been taught that God is a capricious overlord waiting and even wanting to crush human beings like so many ants underfoot.

Other people need freedom from oppressive relationships. They know their lives are controlled not by their heavenly Father, but by a controlling mother, by a boyfriend or girlfriend who is a skilled manipulator, or by a spouse who verbally (or worse, physically) pounds away to gain dominance.

Christ paid the price of our redemption from anyone or anything that has kept us in bondage. Now that we have been redeemed, we must learn how to live in the freedom He has granted. This week, be ruthlessly honest with God: What areas of your life are still chained to an unhealthy behavior, addiction, compulsion or secret sin? Bring into the light what has been hidden in the darkness. You can change a habit in the time it takes to go through this Jubilee experience. If during this time you realize that you need further help and support—reach out! Ask someone at your church for resources. If you realize that you are too closely bound up with another person, use this season to let go of the bonds of control. Lean on God, not on others. Experience the freedom God wants you to have financially, loosed from compulsive spending or selfish greed. Give up perfectionism, selfishness and the need to always be in control. Put the matters of your life into the hands of Christ and begin to experience true freedom.

Crossing the Boundary

The story of the human race begins with freedom. The Genesis story has God saying to Adam, "You are *free* to eat from any tree in the garden . . ." (2:16, emphasis added). In paradise, in a Garden lush and full of life, Adam and Eve were free to consume any of the blessings hanging ripe around them. They were free to take from any tree in the garden . . . except one: "But you must not eat from the tree of the knowledge of good and evil, for when you eat of it you will surely die" (v. 16).

Like a sign that says "WET PAINT–DO NOT TOUCH," human attention is attracted to what we are told we cannot have. Here is the delight and the dilemma of freedom: When God redeems us, we are given the freedom to choose what is healthy and honorable and important. We are free to develop good friendships, to speak to family members in ways that build them up, to volunteer for a meaningful project, to travel to interesting places. But instead, our attention is so often focused on the "WET PAINT" sign, the boundary between what freedom allows and what it does not.

A manager runs his office like his own personal fiefdom, taking advantage of others, keeping subordinates held down so that he can stay on top.

A mother and father use guilt and manipulation on their grown-up children in order to get attention and favors from them. Two of their kids cut them off entirely, but one gets sucked into the vortex of emotional entrapment for years.

A multinational corporation that spends millions on public relations projects a positive and philanthropic image to the public, while in hidden corners of the world, their profits come from the exploitation of child laborers.

A woman separates from her philandering husband, threatening divorce after she discovers one more in a string of serial affairs. But he uses his status and wealth to bleed her with legal fees, while he carries on whatever he wants to.

The story can be told many times over and in many different ways, but the heart of it is always the same: Someone uses his or her freedom to cross a boundary that should not be crossed, and takes away someone else's freedom.

One of the reasons the Exodus from Egypt is such an enduring symbol of hope is that God refused to allow His people to live without their freedom, at the mercy of a tyrant, any longer. God told the children of Abraham that He saw their predicament and heard their cry for help. His liberating response to them assures us that even though this world will only be healed of all its brokenness when it is remade, God *does* liberate people in the here and now. And that's good news! There are people around the world waiting for an Exodus, and each of us will have numerous times in our lives when we need God to lead us out of bondage and into freedom.

The Exodus is God's mark in history. Exodus is what God does; it is what He wills. He is a God who stands for freedom and wants people to come to a place in life where they can thrive. And so His mandate comes: In the Year of Jubilee, all slaves are to be released. Leviticus 25:38-42 says:

> I am the LORD your God, who brought you out of Egypt to give you the land of Canaan and to be your God. If one of your countrymen becomes poor among you and sells himself to you, do not make him work as a slave. He is to be treated as a hired worker or a temporary resident among you; he is to work for you until the Year of Jubilee. Then he and his children are to be released, and he will go back to his own clan and to the property of his forefathers. Because the Israelites are my servants, whom I brought out of Egypt, they must not be sold as slaves.

The Year of Jubilee was a time to remember and reassert everyone's God-given freedom. In the era of the Old Testament, many people sold themselves into slavery. They had no other option if they fell into abject poverty, with no welfare system and no Social Security. The law of Leviticus stipulates that though people, out of necessity, sold themselves into bonded servitude, they were not to be treated as slaves—and in the Year of Jubilee, they were to be forgiven any outstanding debt and allowed to go free.

This was a remarkable opportunity in a day and age when powerful people took cruel advantage of the poor, using their vast resources and power to override the freedom God intended for everyone. Like that enticing "WET PAINT" sign, many people found dominance and oppression incredibly tempting.

It would be encouraging to think that the Israelites obeyed Leviticus 25, but it seems as though they had trouble. They were tempted, like so many others, to cross the boundary and take what was not theirs. Centuries later, the prophet Jeremiah had this oracle for the powerful: "This is what the LORD says: You have not obeyed me; you have not proclaimed freedom for your fellow countrymen. So I now proclaim 'freedom' for you . . . 'freedom' to fall by the sword, plague and famine" (34:17).

They were taken captive by their refusal to set their brothers and sisters free.

Liberation on J-Day

God would not allow human beings to only enjoy their own freedom and not give it to others, so on "J-Day" in that Nazareth synagogue, the first words Jesus read from the scroll were a proclamation of freedom:

> The Spirit of the Lord is on me, because he has anointed me to preach good news to the poor. He has sent me to proclaim freedom for the prisoners and recovery of sight for the blind, to release the oppressed (Luke 4:18).

How exactly did Jesus do all that? His ministry had two basic aspects: *teaching* and *signs.*

The signs, or miracles, dramatically illustrated the freedom that had come with the age of the Messiah. Jesus cast demons out of people, which has got to be the most dramatic example of freedom and liberation. That's exactly what you want to happen to evil—for it to be cast out with divine velocity! (Think about the most evil deeds of the most wicked people today and consider that if they were to allow the power of God into their lives, the demonic would disappear like a mist. You and I need that power and that assurance today. Whether you sense the wickedness of evil close at hand or not, the tempter is always just a step away. He is the accuser. He is the warden of a prison of spiritual defeat.)

When Jesus healed people, He was liberating them from their weaknesses, diseases and disabilities. He didn't heal everybody, just enough people so that the world could know that one day, all would be free from infirmity in the re-creation of all things.

When Jesus forgave people their sins—a miracle even greater than casting out demons or restoring sight to the blind—He was freeing prisoners. There is no greater bondage than to be tied to the guilt of your wrongdoings forever. (Here is where we should be crystal clear about what it means to become a Christian. When you hear the message that Jesus of Nazareth came and proclaimed the opportunity for anybody anywhere to be released from the guilt of their sin—to be forgiven once and for all—and when that goes from a thought, to a possibility, to a reality . . . then you are counted among His followers.)

Jesus' teaching, as well as His signs, released the oppressed. He announced a new and different kingdom—the kingdom of God. Becoming a citizen of the new Kingdom meant that a tyrant could never take away your God-given freedom. This is what Jesus meant when He looked Pontius Pilate in the eye and said, "My kingdom is not of this world" (John 18:36). If Pilate had been at all spiritually perceptive that day, his blood would have run cold.

In Jesus, all the Jubilee themes tie together. The great *Shabbat* began with His coming. His proclamation centered on redemption, and because of the redemption provided by His sacrifice, we are given freedom, which is a consequence of forgiveness and leads to healing and motivates us toward justice.

J-Day indeed.

Where There Is No Freedom

The freedom Christ brings, no matter our circumstances, is the sturdy backbone of believers who face oppression and persecution in many hostile areas in the world. There are few stories more dramatic than the bold witness of believers in China.

A few years ago I was with a group of Christian leaders from North America, visiting some churches in the heartland of China. One Sunday I had the privilege of speaking to a church that was packed from side to side, front to back, with well over 1,000 worshipers. When I arrived that morning, the congregation was already singing, filling the room with sounds that to my ears were strange—but I could recognize in them the universal human cry of praise and petition.

The Communist Revolution, led by Mao Tse-tung who ruled China for a long 27 years, brought with it a barren, atheistic worldview that was widespread by mid-century. According to the communists, God could be replaced by the state (and, practically speaking, by the strong-arm militancy of the state).

Christian missionaries from the West were expelled. Christian faith was suppressed. Yet it was during the Cultural Revolution of 1966 to 1976 that the real oppression began. Every church building was closed. Mao's Red Guards dismantled all the structures of Catholic and Protestant Christianity in China.

Christian leaders were imprisoned, tortured and killed. The literature of the Christians, including the Bible, was destroyed. The outside world wondered what would happen to the Christians so targeted and suppressed by the hostile Chinese state. Would Christianity survive Red China?

When the door came open again after the Cultural Revolution, the world was stunned to discover that the number of Christians had not dwindled but exploded. Whereas there had been one million Christians in China in the middle of the twentieth century, there were now tens of millions. But how could it have happened? There was no Billy Graham of China, no flashy Christian magazines or media networks. In spite of oppression and persecution, Christians in China had continued to meet in homes, forests and fields, and had been active in evangelism, knowing that the government would be hostile either way.

In 1979, a network of officially recognized churches was permitted to open, while the underground house churches continued to develop along the networks they had established during the dark years. Today, no one knows for sure how many Christians are in China. Estimates range from 40 million to 100 million (with numerous informed sources estimating the number to be between 50 million and 70 million). You have to admit that even the low estimates represent a true miracle.

China's story offers more to us than inspiration. The story of Christians in China, and countless other stories of unyielding faith, remind us that *we can be free even where there is no freedom.* We can have the freedom of Christ even while we continue to work for a belligerent boss or to endure a conflict-ridden marriage, or when we have not yet overcome an addiction to alcohol or pornography. The freedom of Christ *can* shake loose the bonds of oppressive personal sins and repressive social structures, but even when that is slow to happen, Christians can live in the wide-open spiritual spaces of redemption and forgiveness. And no one can take away that freedom.

Freedom that Works

We cherish freedom as a gift from God, but why is it that we have such a difficult time handling freedom when we have it?

A young man turns 21 and now has new freedom—legal rights that should be seen as privilege and honor—but he turns it into a spree of illegal and dangerous behavior.

A young man and woman get married, giving them an opportunity to flourish in a new God-given garden of responsibility and pleasure, but instead they begin a protracted battle just weeks after the blessed event, locked in a struggle for territorial power not essentially different from the Israeli-Palestinian conflict.

A woman finally has the courage to leave a long-time abusive relationship, but instead of addressing the patterns in her life that lead her to seek out abuse, she falls into another relationship headed down the same path.

Why doesn't freedom always work? Why can't a tiger held in the captivity of a zoo be released into the wild to flourish among his wild-born cousins? Why is it likely that he'll languish and die?

Here is an important distinction: Freedom is not just freedom *from restraint*; freedom is freedom *to do what God has empowered you to do*. The person who is released from prison may step out with a lightness in his step, gazing at the clear sky above and the distant horizon instead of concrete walls. He is free. Free from prison. *But free to do what?* The rate of recidivism among ex-convicts is as high as it is because many don't know what to do except what they used to do. If the same thing happens to us spiritually, you can see what a disaster it will be.

It isn't enough for a person to find that Jesus Christ will forgive his or her sins and experience the broken chains that come with redemption; that is where grace begins, but hardly where it ends. God wants us not just to be redeemed from sin, but to be free to live good and healthy lives and to be agents of freeing others. God didn't forgive us our sins so that we could go on sinning, but so that we could *be free*. First Peter 2:16 says, "Live as free people, but do not use your freedom as a cover-up for evil; live as servants of God."

A person may get free from alcohol or drug addiction, but what will take the place of the demons that have been exorcized? Jesus was very clear: When one demon has been cast out, there are seven others waiting in line to take its place (see Luke 11:24-26). But 2 Corinthians 3:17-18 says:

> Now the Lord is the Spirit, and where the Spirit of the Lord is, there is freedom. And we, who with unveiled faces all reflect the Lord's glory, are being transformed into his likeness with ever-increasing glory, which comes from the Lord, who is the Spirit.

This passage refers to Moses coming down Mt. Sinai after being in the presence of God with a veil over his face so that the people wouldn't be superstitiously captivated by the radiance of his face. But since Christ, God lifts the veil from all of us who live in His presence. He says, "Look at My Son, be transfixed by who He is and be transformed yourself. Show My glory in your life, an ever-increasing glory. And then you will know what it is to be free. Where My Spirit is, there is freedom."

Transformation is what we're looking for. Nothing less will do. Freedom that merely lets us off the hook for wrong things we've done puts us in no position to prevent those same things from happening again. But when we are *transformed* by freedom, we are free to live as new creations.

Set Free for What?

Why has Christ set us free? *To be free* (see Galatians 5:1). The passage goes on to say, don't "let yourselves be burdened again by a yoke of slavery," because "you were called to be free." Paul says that we must at all costs avoid taking our Christian faith and going backward to a system of laws and regulations. We are called to grown-up faith.

People have had fun collecting some of the inane instructions on consumer products from manufacturers that must think we are idiots. Instructions on sleeping pills: "Warning: May cause drowsiness." On a package of Christmas lights: "Warning: for indoor or outdoor use only." On a pepper spray canister: "Caution: Never aim spray at your own eyes."

God does not treat us like idiots, nor does He treat us like toddlers. Instead, He calls us to grown-up faith. It is for freedom that Christ has set us free. And where Scripture talks elsewhere about "the law that gives freedom" (see James 1:25; 2:12), it is talking about a force in life that is ever-present. As the "law" of gravity and the "laws" of thermodynamics describe inevitable forces in the physical world, the law of Jesus, the law of love and truth, keeps working on us, making us ever freer until that final day when the whole creation will be freed (see Romans 8:21). No more earthquakes. No more tsunamis. No more wars. No more disease. No more death. No more tears.

Both our present, expanding freedom and our future freedom come at a cost—the cost of the cross of Christ and the cost of releasing things that keep us in bondage. Here are some practical steps toward greater freedom:

Boldly Ask God to Show Any Bondage in Your Life

Bondage of the body (addictions, compulsions) often requires the support and counsel of others. Bondage of the mind (small-mindedness, prejudice) is harder to admit because we all think we are reasonable people. Bondage of the spirit (discouragement, depression) is often the most damaging—none of us is meant to live with an empty or broken heart, and we are prone to bind ourselves in body or mind if our spiritual bondage is not broken. In any case, freedom begins with admitting our bondage, and then reaching out to God and others.

Give Up Every Trace of Self-righteousness

We all want to feel good about our standing with God, and that means we are tempted to find something we can be proud of. But that is often the first step toward legalism or hubris—and then we have not only lost our own freedom, we are very likely to impinge on the freedom of others.

Let Go of Anybody You Are Taking Advantage Of

If we want to be really free, we will ask ourselves where we are taking freedom away from somebody else. We let go of resentment because grudges are like chains we put around other people (and ourselves). We treat others with fairness, giving up the advantages of being a ruthless winner in a world where "Might makes right!" is often the only rule people live by. Freeing others is the only way we can be free.

Day 15

Then the land will yield its fruit, and you will eat your fill and live there in safety. You may ask, "What will we eat in the seventh year if we do not plant or harvest our crops?" I will send you such a blessing in the sixth year that the land will yield enough for three years.

LEVITICUS 25:19-21

It is very hard for us to step away from our normal patterns of life, to choose to say, "I am going to stop (*shavat*) so that I can take in what God has done in the past, what He is doing around me now and what He might do in the future." It is especially hard to do if you fear you'll lose something in the transaction.

In the same way, it was a challenge for the Israelites when God told them to take a Year of Jubilee and let the land lie fallow (to translate for those who don't live on farms, "fallow" means to plant no crops and let the land rest). *What? You want us to do what? Not plant for a whole year? Not coax grain out of the fields, fill our barns, feel secure and make a profit?* And God said, "Yes, that's exactly what I want you to do. And there is one main reason for it—*freedom*."

One of the things that can keep us in bondage is the belief that unless we keep running as hard as we're running or earning as much as we're earning, life will fall apart. The Sabbath years were faith testers and faith builders for God's people.

These years were God's way of getting the people's attention, like looking a distraught person directly in the eye and speaking words that are strong, true and reassuring.

A harvest of thick shocks of grain is a good thing. For us to earn a paycheck, be able to put food on the table and have some left over for entertainment is a good thing. But God wants us to know that our security does not rest on what we have in the bank or what we've stored in the basement. He invites us to put the sickle down, stop clenching our teeth, cease being stressed-out by fear of not having enough, appreciate His blessings and enjoy the freedom.

Make It Real: Okay, let's get very tangible. Look in your wallet right now and see what you have. Decide on a portion of that amount that you will give away anonymously today as an act of grace to someone else. As you do so, thank God for the opportunity to be a channel of His blessing and for the freedom that comes with giving.

Day 16

It is for freedom that Christ has set us free. Stand firm, then, and do not let yourselves be burdened by a yoke of slavery.

GALATIANS 5:1

A *tautology* is a statement that seems unnecessary because it says the same thing twice, such as "I quit my job so I wouldn't have to work there anymore." Galatians 5:1 appears to be a tautology: "It is for freedom that Christ has set us free." When someone is set free, aren't they free? Not necessarily. Before we glance over it as if it is stating the obvious, we should stop and wonder why the apostle Paul said it.

Galatians 5 talks about a bondage to the Law, enslavement to the belief that we can achieve a truce with God our Creator if we follow all the rules just right, make visible displays of righteousness and track all our spiritual accomplishments. That is the way of Pharisees, and Paul had had enough of it. Before his conversion he was really good at it, but after he met Jesus on the road to Damascus and experienced true freedom, he saw only spiritual death in the way of the Law.

A convict can be set free but still think like a convict, talk like a convict and behave like a convict: constricted, suppressed and afraid. Like a person who lived for a long time in a controlling, abusive relationship, he or she may go on cowering in life even when the oppression is gone.

The laws of the Old Testament are good. The Ten Commandments have ongoing relevance. But when Jesus came—Jesus, who is the Jubilee and liberates us from every form of bondage—everything changed. He demonstrated that while the Law was necessary to teach the human race the difference between right and wrong, *He* brought grace and truth. By God's mercy through Jesus, we are allowed to repent and turn to God for a whole new life. He frees us from the childish way of following "dos" and "don'ts" so that we can freely live in obedience to Christ. We do what is right because we are right with God and our instincts have been realigned with who He is.

But we must remember that we are free. We must rehearse it. Any person can become a Pharisee on any given day. We can turn faith into performance, like a kid trying to gain Mom or

Dad's favor by being a star player on the soccer field.

No. It is for freedom that Christ has set us free.

Make It Real: Write out this phrase from Galatians 5:1 on a piece of paper—IT IS FOR FREEDOM THAT CHRIST HAS SET US FREE—and tape it to a mirror you use regularly. Every time you look in the mirror today, reflect on that truth.

Day 17

He and his children are to be released, and he will go back to his own clan and to the property of his forefathers. Because the Israelites are my servants, whom I brought out of Egypt, they must not be sold as slaves.

LEVITICUS 25:41-42

Everybody must have looked forward to the Year of Jubilee. In some way, each person experienced freedom. No one was more dramatically affected, however, than the slave. Imagine being told one day that a new season had come: "You can go back home."

Slavery was a simple fact of the ancient world. It was virtually universal. It may seem as though some passages in the Bible endorse slavery, but Scripture gradually and progressively picks away at the underpinnings of slavery—not all at once, but as a step-by-step retraining of the human race. The Old Testament, for instance, holds that people living as slaves are still people, made in the image of God; they are not property and must not be treated as animals. In a world that viewed slaves as little more than beasts of burden, this position was incredibly radical.

Jubilee was a time when Israelites who had found it necessary to sell themselves into bonded servitude were freed. They could go back home. These were people who were so poor that the only way they could survive was to throw themselves in complete dependence on a wealthier family. In such a position, they survived—but they were also trapped.

So God said that every 50 years the people were to review this simple truth: *No one is hopelessly trapped.* Slave owners must release their servants, even though it would disrupt the economic structure of their lives. The Year of Jubilee was a time when dignity was restored.

A famous poem concludes with the words, "You can't go home again"—you can't turn back the hands of time and you can't gain back what you've grown beyond. But that is not true spiritually. You *can* go back to a more innocent day. You *can* return to a simpler way of life. You *can* regain your purity or renew your faithful vows of marriage even if you've strayed. You *can* get out of debt. You *can* grow past resentment. You *can* remove yourself from someone's oppressive voice in your life.

God wants you back home.

Make It Real: Today, whenever you leave your house or come back to it, take a few moments to thank God that life can change, that there are second chances and fresh starts. Thank Him that you can go home again.

Day 18

He has sent me to proclaim freedom for the prisoners.
LUKE 4:18

The chemicals for the lethal injection were about to be released down the lines and into the arm of Karla Faye Tucker, who was strapped to a gurney in the execution room of Huntsville Penitentiary in Texas. Her last words were: "I love all of you very much. . . . I am going to be face to face with Jesus now. Warden Baggett, thank all of you so much. You have been so good to me. I love all of you very much. I will see you all when you get there. I will wait for you."[1]

The liquid flowed and her body was poisoned. She was the first woman executed in the state of Texas since the Civil War. Karla Faye never denied the heinous crime that had put her in prison. In a drug-crazed state, she had followed her boyfriend to the house of a drug dealer, and they killed the man and a woman sharing his bed with a pickaxe.

She was on death row for 14 years, and when she came to believe in Christ during that time, she went through a personal transformation that was contagious to everyone who had contact with her. She went into prison one person and exited another. She understood her guilt and understood her freedom in Christ. Fellow prisoners, workers at the prison and people all over the country were influenced by her vibrant faith.

She sent a poem to a fellow prisoner just before her execution: "God wanted to plant a flower in a harsh and barren place. So He found a warped seedling, rejected by the human race. Men said the plant was hopeless, but He reached down deep inside, replacing its horrible evil with His love so deep and wide."[2]

We put people in prisons—an unfortunate necessity—to take away their freedom. But that will never stop someone from finding Christ and claiming the freedom He came to provide.

Make It Real: Pray today for someone you have been tempted to give up on or a situation that has not changed in many years. Ask God to give you hope for that person or situation, and faith in His liberating promises.

Day 19

But thanks be to God that, though you used to be slaves to sin, you wholeheartedly obeyed the form of teaching to which you were entrusted. You have been set free from sin and have become slaves to righteousness.

ROMANS 6:17-18

Three friends on the golf course get into a conversation in which they let their guard down and begin to open up to each other. One discloses that his biggest temptation in life is drinking too much. That leads another friend to reveal that he has had a significant problem with sexual temptations for a long time. They look at the third man and say, "Okay, we've gone pretty far out on a limb. Now it's your turn. You must have some special temptation, some area of vulnerability." The man hesitates and then speaks up: "My biggest temptation is gossip. And I just can't wait to get back so I can talk to somebody."

Sin as a taskmaster is no laughing matter. Lives are torn apart all the time by compulsive patterns and self-destructive behaviors. So when Jesus said that with His coming there would be release for captives, He was talking about every one of us.

It doesn't come naturally or easily for most people to admit that they are captive; most of us want to believe that we are the captains of our own destinies. But just stop and think for a minute about the word "captive." Isn't it true that every one of us at one time or another has found something or someone *captivating*? And if we were captivated long enough, didn't we realize that we had relinquished some of our will to that person, possession or pursuit? Scripture says that when we go our own way, when we hoard our possessions, when we give in to passion or get carried away in rage—we are made captives. We become slaves to sin.

Yet Romans 6 tells us that God has broken us out of Egypt. He has released us to the freedom of a Promised Land, though there is wilderness we must cross to get there. All it takes to begin this journey is to say, "I'd rather have God as my Master than myself. I don't want to live in a cage. I want to be freed by righteousness, and to follow Christ to places I would never believe I could go."

Make It Real: Take 10 minutes today to read Romans 6–8. After you do, get on your knees and reflect on ways that you are a slave to sin. Maybe you're a slave to greed or jealousy, pride or gluttony. As you pray about these things, praise God that He has freed you to come under the mastery of righteousness.

Day 20

So then, I myself in my mind am a slave to God's law, but in the sinful nature a slave to the law of sin.

ROMANS 7:25

Millions of people have begun the road to recovery from alcoholism and substance abuse by following the guidelines known as the "Twelve Steps." Alcoholics Anonymous was founded in the 1950s by two men known as Bill W. and Dr. Bob. The real genius behind the program, however, was the pastor of Calvary Episcopal Church in New York, Reverend Sam Shoemaker. Calvary Church ran a rescue mission, and Reverend Shoemaker found that the only way to break the bondage of alcoholism was through a rigorous process of self-examination, acknowledgement of personal culpability, dependence on God and prayer, and a commitment to restitution for harm done.[3] While the Twelve Steps are not a biblical theology of change per se, it is clear that they are based in biblical values. It takes a leap of faith to begin this process:

1. Admit that you are powerless over alcohol—that your life has become unmanageable.
2. Believe that a Power greater than yourself could restore you to sanity.
3. Make a decision to turn your will and your life over to the care of God as you understand Him.
4. Make a searching and fearless moral inventory of yourself.
5. Admit to God, to yourself and to another human being the exact nature of your wrongs.

6. Be ready to have God remove all these defects of character.
7. Humbly ask God to remove your shortcomings.
8. Make a list of all persons you have harmed and become willing to make amends to them all.
9. Make amends to such people wherever possible, except when to do so would injure them or others.
10. Continue to take personal inventory, and when you are wrong, promptly admit it.
11. Seek through prayer and meditation to improve your conscious contact with God, as you understand Him, praying only for knowledge of His will for you and the power to carry that out.
12. Having had a spiritual awakening as the result of these steps, carry this message to alcoholics and practice these principles in all your affairs.[4]

It is not surprising that the Twelve Steps have been applied to many other oppressive and compulsive life behaviors and helped people begin to live in freedom. As Romans 7 says, there are certain "laws" at work in our lives, and dependency on God is the only way to true freedom.

Make It Real: Underline two of the Twelve Steps above that have some application to your life circumstances right now. Spend some time today thinking and praying about how you can follow through on those Steps.

Day 21

Consecrate the fiftieth year and proclaim liberty throughout the land to all its inhabitants.

LEVITICUS 25:10

If you go to the city of Philadelphia today, you can visit a historic eighteenth-century building that contains a room called Independence Hall. This ordinary room was the place where, on July 4, 1776, the Declaration of Independence was signed and where, in 1787, the Constitution of the United States was drafted. A huge bell, which we know as the Liberty Bell, hung in the bell tower there. Inscribed on its side are the words of Moses written 3,000 years earlier, declaring a Year of Jubilee: "Proclaim liberty throughout the land to all its inhabitants" (Leviticus 25:10).

The bell in that tower was rung before the first public reading of the Declaration of Independence, as it had been before other important occasions. But the bell became an icon decades later when it was depicted on the cover of a new magazine called *Liberty*, a publication devoted to the cause of the abolition of slavery. The publishers of that magazine believed that freedom in this new nation was not just freedom from the taxes of the king of England; it had to be freedom for every man and woman, boy and girl—the freedom that is the God-endowed dignity of the human race.

In the Year of Jubilee, the Israelites were supposed to let their slaves go free—a hint that one day slavery would be abolished altogether. When God told the Israelites that they should observe a Year of Jubilee every fiftieth year, one of His purposes was to teach the people again that He, the living God, stood for freedom. We know that liberty is important to God because the Bible talks again and again about the Exodus from Egypt as the symbol of His ongoing liberating work in the world.

God knows that we all have taskmasters. One person is enslaved to alcohol or drugs, another to a domineering person. One person is trapped in guilt and shame imposed by others, another is in the bondage of *being* the taskmaster–an addiction to control. There is not a single person who does not need to hear the sound of liberty ring loud and clear through their heart and mind. And only the living God can deliver that kind of liberty.

Make It Real: Think about the forces at work in your life that hold you in a kind of bondage and write these down. Take a few minutes to pray seriously for God to release you. Pray with the confidence that God is able and willing to do so. As you experience redemption in these areas, don't forget to thank the God who redeems!

Notes

1. "Karla Faye Tucker" at Wikipedia.org. http://en.wikipedia.org/wiki/Karla_Faye_Tucker (accessed April 2008).
2. Linda Strom, *Karla Faye Tucker Set Free* (Colorado Springs, CO: Shaw Books, 2000), p. 50.
3. Dick B., "Rev. Sam Shoemaker, A.A.: 'Co-founder' and Spiritual Source," from Anonymous One. http://www.anonymousone.com/faq63.htm (accessed April 2008).
4. "The Twelve Steps of Alcoholics Anonymous," from 12step.org. http://www.12step.org/Versions-of-the-12-Steps.html (accessed April 2008).

WEEK 3

GROUP DISCUSSION QUESTIONS

1. "Freedom" is a word used frequently in our stories, in our politics and in our daily lives. What does the average person think of when the topic of freedom is raised? What do you think of when you hear the word "freedom"?

2. What are some forms of bondage that people get themselves into?

3. What kinds of personal bondage have the most destructive effect in people's lives? In your life?

4. What is an area of life in which you long to have greater freedom?

5. It is commonly said that our three great enemies are sin, death and Satan. In what ways can each of these have a binding effect in our lives?

6. In what ways have you seen the liberating power of Christ?

7. How does forgiveness become a liberating force in our lives?

8. Inscribed on the Liberty Bell are the words of Jubilee: "Proclaim liberty throughout the land . . ." How can you proclaim liberty to the people in your life?

WEEK 4

FORGIVENESS

Accepting the Mercy of God and Letting Go of Those You've Held in Debt

I knew that Jerry had a dramatic story of personal forgiveness that needed to be shared with a wide audience, so one weekend when I was going to speak on the topic, I asked him to share his story with our whole church. It seems like it's always hardest to forgive the people who are closest to us—a brother, a daughter, a friend—and Jerry had experienced one of the most difficult: forgiving his mother. What could be harder than to forgive a mother who had abandoned you?

Jerry grew up in a broken home. That's difficult enough, but on top of that reality, neither his father nor his mother wanted to take custody of him when their marriage broke up. At a very young age, a court assigned Jerry's care to an aunt.

The damage of those early years showed up in college, when depression and hopelessness came over him like a dark cloud. One day he found himself desperately trying to win back a girlfriend over the phone, telling her that if she didn't come back to him, he would take his own life with his shotgun in the closet. (Now Jerry can say with some humor that he does not recommend this as a way of regaining a relationship.) She hung up the phone and called the police, who quickly swept down on Jerry's room.

Bitterness toward his mom held Jerry in bondage for many years. When he discovered she had "found God" at a church and had given her life over to Him, Jerry was more bitter than ever. *How can she receive God's forgiveness when I'm not ready to forgive her?* But over the years, as Jerry's own faith developed, he came finally to the place of releasing his mother from her debt of rejection and abandonment.

What neither Jerry nor I knew when I asked him to share is that his mother would die just a couple of days before the Sunday he was scheduled to speak. We told him he didn't have to speak under such distressing circumstances, but he insisted on it. He wanted to tell thousands of other people about how he had forgiven his mother and how they had been reconciled—even if he had to do it barely 24 hours after her funeral.

Forgiveness is all about freedom. Forgiveness is an offer of freedom to the wrongdoer, and a claiming of freedom for the forgiver.

I get more of a reaction from people when I speak about forgiveness than almost any other topic, and I've frequently asked people why that might be. What I've learned is that nearly everyone knows what it feels like either to hold a grudge or to be unforgiven: absolutely terrible. If we don't know that we are forgiven and if we don't have the ability or will to forgive others, we go through life with a burden of guilt and regret on our backs that feels as if we are carrying a decomposing corpse. Or it can feel like a burning in the gut that does not warm, but smolders and eats away at us. Or it can feel like being lost in a lonely ocean, tossed about by confused and confusing waves. No wonder we want forgiveness, and no wonder we want to learn how to forgive.

That's how unforgiveness feels, but horrible feelings are the least of it. Forgiveness and unforgiveness are objective realities. Lack of forgiveness is a burden, a fire or a lostness because it is the severing of relationship, and we humans are made to be connected in relationships. Unforgiveness creates an impassible barrier between people who are meant to be together. Forgiveness, on the other hand, builds a bridge that strengthens and deepens the connection between them.

Forgiveness is one of the underlying themes of Jubilee because the "good news" and the "freedom" and "the LORD's favor" and the "comfort" mentioned in Jesus' synagogue reading on J-Day (see Luke 4, hearkening back to Isaiah 61) are not just about external life circumstances. Redemption works and freedom happens when God releases us from the bondage of our guilt—when He forgives us.

Forgiveness Is *Not* . . .

I don't know how many times I've heard from someone that he or she reconnected with a parent who was on his or her deathbed and that it was one of the best things to ever happen in that person's life. Grown men go to their dad's deathbed with the slim hope that the father will reach out his hand and say: "I'm sorry for the mistakes I've made . . . will you forgive me?"

I have also met many people who are skeptical of forgiveness. They don't think they need to be forgiven by anybody (they're not axe murderers, after all!), and they're not inclined to forgive those people who have done them wrong. Why let other people off the hook? Why call something that was wrong, right? But when we choose the road of unforgiveness, the burden and the burning and the drifting continue—and we often choose it because we don't understand the true meaning of forgiveness.

But before getting to what forgiveness *is*, let's start with what forgiveness is *not*.

Forgiveness is *not* a compromise of morality. Don't ever think that God would confuse moral clarity and moral responsibility with grace and forgiveness. God is not "soft." God is love, and that means that He is good and just. God's justice ensures that the murderer will not get away with murder, the sex offender will not get away with molestation, and the liar will not—in the end—get away with lies. Now of course, people do "get away with things" all the time. But bad behavior has a way of catching up with us down the road, even if it is not until the Day of Judgment. Forgiveness is *not* a violation of moral justice. God, because of His very nature, could never compromise that.

Forgiveness is *not* merely the avoidance of conflict. There are a lot of us who do not like conflict. We don't want to have hard feelings or hard words with someone else, so we skirt around disagreements and disunity. Some people may appear to be forgiving, but because they are merely avoiding conflict, they are seething on the inside while smiling on the outside. Worse yet, resentment may turn rotten inside them, and everything good becomes tainted. Sometimes forbearing is the right thing to do, but avoidance of conflict is not the same thing as forgiveness.

Forgiveness Is . . . Release

Try for a moment to forget everything you have ever heard about forgiveness. Forget about remorse and pleading and guilt.

Set aside any scene that comes to mind when forgiveness is mentioned. If you do so, then one simple, clear concept can shape your thinking on forgiveness.

The biblical idea of forgiveness is unambiguous, demonstrated by the Greek word *aphesis* used in the New Testament, which means "release." To forgive means to choose to let someone whom you have been holding on to—holding in your debt, holding in resentment and bitterness, holding in obligation—go. To release him or her.

Let that word sink deeply in: *release*. It is the key to understanding forgiveness. Imagine yourself gripping something tightly with your hand, so tightly that your knuckles turn white and your fingers begin to ache. And then you let go. You release.

Forgiveness is not calling someone's immoral or destructive action okay. It is not turning a blind eye to injustice. Forgiveness simply means that you choose to release somebody from personal obligation to you, knowing that the person will have to face the justice of God.

The speed limit on the road from my house to my office is 25 mph. It used to be 35. The road is semi-residential . . . and it is downhill. So you can imagine (I hope you can), that it is very easy for me, driving that same route hundreds of times a year, to drive somewhat over the speed limit (I won't say what I mean by "somewhat"). One day, I was driving that route and I noticed colors in my rearview mirror. Flashy red and blue lights—striking at first, then ominous. I got that empty-pit feeling in my stomach as I saw those condemning lights and heard the squad car blasting its accusing siren. I pulled over to the side. I rolled down my window. The police officer sauntered toward my car (why do they walk so slowly?). With each step he took, the chimes of condemnation echoed in my head: "Guilty! Guilty! Guilty!" When he got to my window, he asked if I knew this was a 25 mile per hour zone and requested to see my driver's license. "Yes, sir," I said, my voice suddenly half an octave higher than normal. He strolled back to his car.

I think the officer was in his car long enough to have his lunch, but when he finally lumbered back to my door and handed me my license, he used words that were so good, so gracious. He told me that I had exceeded the speed limit on Barker Road, but that he was going to give me a warning this time. *A warning.* Those were the words I wanted to hear. And then he released me and wandered back to his car.

Release. The concept is simple and clear, and it is the biblical meaning of forgiveness. Forgiveness is not saying that something wrong is now right. It is not moral compromise. It is not letting someone get away with something. It is an intentional decision to release someone from obligation to you.

In Matthew 18, we read that Jesus' disciple Peter asks Him, "How many times shall I forgive my brother when he sins against me? Up to seven times?" (v. 21).

Jesus answers with a parable. In His story, a man owed a king ten thousand talents (today's equivalent would be millions of dollars). He was on the brink of having to sell his wife and children into slavery to pay the debt, but the man pleaded with the king and his debt was cancelled. *Forgiven. Released.* But the same man, as he left the king's presence where he was forgiven his mammoth debt, turned on a man who owed him merely a hundred *denarii* ($20 or so). When the king heard of it, he was incensed and said, "You wicked servant, I canceled all that debt of yours. Shouldn't you have had mercy on your fellow servant?" The king's forgiveness was rescinded (vv. 23-34).

Jesus' closing words are these: "This is how my heavenly Father will treat each of you unless you forgive your brother from your heart" (v. 35).

Forgiveness is release. When we are released by God, we are able to release other people in our lives.

Forgiveness Is . . . the Application of Grace and Truth

On October 2, 2006, America was stunned to hear of a shooting rampage in a schoolhouse. A man had entered a simple one-room school building in an Amish community in Pennsylvania, and before he left, the blood of five girls, ages 7 to 13, and himself was soaking into the wooden floor.

Beyond the brutality of the tragedy, what really shocked the nation was hearing in the days that followed that the Amish community had decided "to forgive" the killer. How could that be? How could people in an Amish community begin to talk about forgiveness within a day or two of a murderer having cut down their children? Was it that they don't care about their children? Was it that they don't have it in them to be indignant over an act of unspeakable cruelty?

No. The Amish did not soften the judgment of God on the cruelty of a man who stole children from their parents; they just knew that judgment was not theirs to bestow. The gunman was dead at his own hand. He had exited this life. He would stand before the judgment of God. The man's wife and children, on the other hand, so cruelly left behind, did not need to be punished in his absence. The Amish community saw that they needed love, not ostracism . . . and they loved them.

John 1:14 says that Jesus came to us "full of grace and truth." That is how we know that the mercy of forgiveness is not a compromise of the firmness of justice. Grace and truth coexist, and they do so most fully in Jesus. When a tornado whips through the lives of those who are deeply rooted in the grace and truth of Christ, they are able to stand. They don't let evil turn them evil. Rather than be blown away, they cling to God's grace and truth in the storm.

The Amish have a deep faith in the providence of God, a knowledge that God is there even when tragedy strikes. They have seen evil before; their European ancestors were sometimes mercilessly persecuted for their faith—burned at the stake or drowned in rivers. They have seen evil raise its ugly face before. And the Amish have a strong bond of community. That makes all the difference in the world. When tragedy hits, and you know you are not alone, you have the moral strength to be able to stand up in the face of evil and apply the grace and truth of God.

Forgiveness Is . . . a New Way of Looking at Others

If we believe that God forgives, even though He is not obligated to, and that we have the best kind of life when we hold people in our lives with a loose grip, then we will see others for who they can be and who they are intended to be rather than simply as they are. As this happens, we will find that there are fewer and fewer people who simply irritate us. Of course, if we choose to, we can focus on the traits and habits in others that irritate us most (and end up irritating the living daylights out of everyone around us). Likewise, we can choose to condemn people who commit the most heinous of crimes, seeing only the horrifying deeds they have done, not who God created them to be. But it doesn't have to be that way.

Forgiveness is a new way of looking at others. It's a radical and counter-cultural perspective on relating to people. Forgiveness means seeing those who have wronged us as God sees them, rather than considering only how their actions and characteristics irritate or inconvenience us. And forgiveness means that we view the deranged people who shoot up school rooms and then turn the gun on themselves as people created in God's image who are now standing before the judgment seat of God, answering to Him.

When we choose to forgive, our "me-colored" glasses are removed and we begin to see people as they really are.

Forgiveness Is . . . a Process

Forgiveness is a choice but it is also a process. You can release someone from their obligation even as the smoldering fires of resentment keep burning in you for some time to come. This is important to keep in mind, because some people who really want to forgive those who have hurt them agonize that they cannot yet forget the wrong. The wound has not healed. It stings.

We need to be very careful with the concept of "forgive and forget." Forgiving means to choose to release someone from obligation to you, but what happens when you can't forget that big blowup or that betrayal or that infidelity? Does that mean that you haven't really forgiven? No—forgiveness means that we give the gift of releasing, but it does not mean that we suddenly become amnesiacs.

One time, a couple came to talk to me and unfolded a hurtful and messy story. The husband had been away on a business trip just a few months earlier and had done what he thought he would never do: He had drawn too close to a female associate. He came home an adulterer.

Within days, he confessed to his wife what had happened. He knew that he had a marriage worth saving, and he loved his kids. He did not want to give all that up. He wanted to fix things if they could be fixed, and he wanted to make sure that it never happened again.

His wife was devastated, but in the days that followed, she accepted his remorse and repentance as genuine. With the help of a marriage counselor, they began to put the marriage back together and take some practical steps to adultery-proof their relationship. But they came to my office because they didn't know how to make forgiveness a reality. The wife was still, months later, very hurt and angry about the husband's infidelity, and she believed that she must not have really forgiven him—otherwise, she would have forgotten.

I looked at her and asked, "Would you say that today the fires of your resentment are not quite as hot as they were a month ago?"

"Yes," she replied.

"And a month ago, were they not quite as hot as they had been the month before that?"

"Yes."

It was clear to me that this wife, so deeply wounded, had truly released her husband from the guilt of his one-night stand—she had forgiven him—*and* that she was also *in the process of forgiving*. Forgiveness doesn't mean amnesia. Even God, who says, "I will forgive their wickedness and remember their sins no more" (Jeremiah 31:34), does not experience a sudden loss of memory when He forgives us for what has happened in the past. History is history. We need history—the bad chapters often even more than the good ones—to help us chart the best course forward in our lives. When we do forgive and forget, a matter moves from the front of our minds to the far back. We "forget" in the sense that we choose not to make a forgiven matter a tool with which we keep prodding the offender.

How Does Forgiveness Work?

Decide that this is the season of your life to get serious about forgiving people who have hurt you. Make a list of those who have frustrated you, betrayed you or led you into trouble. Cross off a name when you let that person go, releasing him or her to the higher justice of God. Make another list of people you have offended, including members of your immediate family. And ask God to grant His forgiveness for the ways you have offended or betrayed Him, and to show you healing ways to ask forgiveness of others during this Jubilee experience.

We are terribly mistaken if we think that forgiveness is something only certain soft-hearted people are capable of, and the rest of us with harder edges will never get it right. Remember, the boldest act of forgiveness the world has ever seen was in the bloodied and beaten and torn body of Jesus Christ. Nothing soft about that. To forgive is the gutsiest thing you can do in life, and it is not for the faint-hearted. Forgiveness is the mark of the true man and the true woman of God.

But how does it work?

The Responsibility of the Person Seeking Forgiveness

Psalm 32 is a touchstone passage for those who are seeking forgiveness:

> Blessed is he whose transgressions are forgiven, whose sins are covered. Blessed is the man whose sin the LORD does not count against him and in whose spirit is no deceit. When I kept silent, my bones wasted away through my groaning all day long. For day and night your hand was heavy upon me; my strength was sapped as in the heat of summer. Then I acknowledged my sin to you and did not cover up my iniquity. I said, "I will confess my transgressions to the LORD"—and you forgave the guilt of my sin (vv. 1-5).

First, to be forgiven is to be blessed beyond our wildest dreams, knowing that our Creator, the gracious Father above, is willing to forgive our mistakes and offenses. God will not hold our sins against us. Our record is wiped clean. No debt owed. Account settled. We must comprehend the blessing of forgiveness. If, instead, we take God's forgiveness for granted with an attitude that says, "Well, what else is God going to do?

Isn't that His job?" then there is not a chance that we will be forgiving of others.

Notice the progression of the psalm writer's heart in this passage. Early on, he admits that "my bones wasted away . . . my strength was sapped." This is a person being "eaten up on the inside," as we sometimes say. Guilt does that. But then, as his poem progresses, the writer acknowledges that his tortured conscience is a gift, because his misery compels him to turn to God. In our society, we should not be so quick to avoid the bad feelings that come with a guilty conscience. Look at the con-man and the charlatan, look at the terrorist, the spouse-abuser and the chat-room predator, and you see the result when legitimate guilt is ignored: a dead conscience. Be glad that your conscience is alive and making noise, even when it sometimes shouts at you.

When was the last time you tried to cover up your transgressions? We all know cover-ups aren't limited to Washington, DC; covering up is the unfortunate instinct of fallen human nature. Denying our faults and mess-ups seems, in the moment, to be the way of least pain, but avoidance and deceit only add pain on top of pain. Verse 5 tells us about the responsibility of the person seeking forgiveness: "Then I acknowledged my sin to you and did not cover up my iniquity. I said, 'I will confess my transgressions to the LORD'—and you forgave the guilt of my sin."

We must confess our wrongdoings. But to whom? The simple answer is that we should confess to the person or persons we have wronged. In every instance, that is God. In Psalm 51, which is King David's heart-rending confession of his adultery with Bathsheba and his arrangement of the death of her husband, he writes, "Against you, you only, have I sinned" (v. 4). Of course, he had sinned against people, but the epicenter of the earthquake of our sins is always our detachment from God Himself. And so we confess to God.

We also must confess our wrongdoings to the people we've wronged, in most—but not all—circumstances. We must judge the outcome: Will confessing our sins to the people we have wronged deepen our relationship with them and with God, or will it cause even more damage? Saying to your sister-in-law, "You know, I used to resent you all the time because I thought you were arrogant, but I've really learned how to tolerate you and to forgive your many shortcomings" may not be the most relationally constructive thing to do. Likewise, admitting that you are sexually attracted to a married person in your office is a confession best made to God alone, not to your co-worker.

But there are many other times when a flat-out, humble-pie, heartfelt apology is exactly the right thing to do. And if you know its right, don't hold back.

The Responsibility of the Forgiver

The first thing to do when you think you should forgive someone who has wronged you is to make sure that your forgiveness rises to the level of true forgiveness. Colossians 3:13 says, "Bear with each other and forgive whatever grievances you may have against one another. Forgive as the Lord forgave you."

There is *forgiveness* and there is *forbearance*. Think of forbearance as a kind of low-level forgiveness; it is exercising patience with and tolerance of the idiosyncrasies of the people in your life. For example, your spouse's chronic lateness doesn't rise to the level of mortal sin. It may be irritating, but none of the Ten Commandments say, "Thou shalt arrive no less than 10 minutes early to any and all appointments, because 10 minutes early is 5 minutes late." Similarly, good table manners and appropriate social graces didn't make it into God's Top 10.

You may need to forbear with someone who talks too much, someone who wears really pungent perfume, someone who chews with his or her mouth open or who leaves towels on the floor or who seems incapable of replacing the toilet paper roll. You may need to smile and tolerate some of the weird opinions of others—or their lack of opinions or their overabundance of opinions—but that tolerance is more forbearance than forgiveness.

If you don't see the necessity of forbearing (at least on occasion), then you may have a narcissistic mindset. Do you really believe that your way of living and thinking is superior in every way to others'? If you feel as though you should never have to put up with other people's irritating behavior, watch out: You may have a very skewed view of life (and chances are that you're pretty irritating yourself).

We need to live with a firm grasp on the reality that we live in an imperfect world surrounded by imperfect people, and not every bumping of heads means someone has sinned. This is not to say that we should minimize our sins against each other, expecting others to put up with our mess-ups just because "no one is perfect." Real people do real damage to each other, and the only remedy is tough, tender, brave, even risky forgiveness. Let me say it again, because it's worth remembering: *Forgiveness is the gutsiest thing a human being can do.*

Forgiveness is a ministry, not just to the people you forgive, but as an example of a better way to a world that easily lives resentment and revenge (see John 20:23 and 2 Corinthians 2:6-10). This is how the ministry works: When you need to be forgiven (and you know because you're eaten up on the inside), you come clean with God, with yourself, and, in some cases, with the person whom you have offended. If you need to forgive someone else, you draw on the deep well of mercy, confront the problem, let go and then begin the process of forgiveness. Jesus said to go first to the person who has sinned against you, one on one. If after that you are not able to reconcile, you may need to draw other people into a process of confrontation (see Matthew 18:15-18).

Sounds easy, right? The fact is, sometimes forgiveness *is* amazingly easy . . . and sometimes there are huge roadblocks. Bitterness, a toxin for the spirit, can hold us back from forgiveness. Talking to God about what went wrong or with a confidant who can sympathize can help us let go of bitterness.

Vindictiveness is another roadblock. In his book *Freedom of Forgiveness*, David Augsburger writes, "Revenge is the most worthless weapon in the world. It ruins the avenger while more firmly confirming the enemy in his wrong. It initiates an endless flight down a bottomless stairway of rancor, reprisals, and ruthless retaliation."[1]

How Do We Forgive?

Once we have put away bitterness and the impulse toward revenge, how can we get started forgiving?

1. Be Willing

First, we have to be willing to forgive and willing to strive for grace. Micah 7:18 offers this insight into why God forgives: "Who is a God like you, who pardons sin and forgives the transgression of the remnant of his inheritance? You do not stay angry forever but delight to show mercy." God forgives because He *delights* in showing mercy. God does get angry. He does have wrath. But that is not the way He wants things to stay. God delights in showing mercy.

Do we?

Let's be honest: When we release somebody, when we tell him or her that we forgive, do we walk away with steam coming out of our ears or do we feel released as well? If we really have forgiven, we will experience some measure of release, even if the process of forgiveness takes much longer than we expect. If we truly delight in showing mercy, our initial act of forgiveness will be a jumpstart to our process of forgiveness; our wounded hearts will begin to be mended because we are willing to strive for grace.

In Luke 6:35, Jesus sets this high standard of Kingdom living:

> Love your enemies, do good to them, and lend to them without expecting to get anything back. Then your reward will be great, and you will be sons of the Most High, because he is kind to the ungrateful and wicked. Be merciful, just as your Father is merciful. Do not judge, and you will not be judged. Do not condemn, and you will not be condemned. Forgive, and you will be forgiven.

Willingness to forgive is not a grudging obedience to a God who says, "Can't we all just get along?" Being merciful happens—*really* happens—only when we are willing to be (and act like!) the sons and daughters of God that we are, becoming more and more like Him in character and kindness.

2. Strive for Truth

Oftentimes the "letting go" of forgiveness happens only after the truth of a problem has been put squarely on the table. Confronting someone may not come easy for you, but it may be the most merciful thing you can do for someone you care about. Jesus said in Luke 17:3, "If your brother sins, rebuke him, and if he repents, forgive him." In other words, tell the truth to your brother or sister so that reconciliation can begin.

That's the ideal resolution we all hope for: a mistake, a confrontation, an apology and forgiveness. And we *should* hope for the ideal, even as we realize that sometimes we will have to release someone when they are not convinced that they have done anything wrong.

3. Know the Limits of Forgiveness

Jesus' disciple Peter asked Him one day whether there was a maximum number of times he should forgive—maybe seven times? (See Matthew 18:21-22.) Jesus' famous reply—no, not seven times, but seven times seventy—tells us that there is no three-strikes-and-you're-out policy (or seven strikes, as the case may be). If such a policy were the case, we would all be in a heap of trouble—surely each of us has sinned against God far more than seven times.

There *are* limits to the restoration forgiveness can bring if the offender does not admit his or her offense. Let's say that you decide to forgive your brother for having been cruel to you when you were growing up. You've resented him for years, but now you are an adult, you've got kids of your own and you just want to let the past go. You can do that. You can release him. You can tell him that you have been bitter about the past and that you have decided to let the matter go. The hoped-for scenario is that your brother recognizes and admits his offenses against you and is grateful for your forgiveness, and then the two of you are able to move forward in your relationship. But maybe he won't. What if instead his response is "I don't have a clue what you're talking about; anything I dished up years ago you probably deserved"? That certainly takes the joy out of forgiveness, but it doesn't stop you from releasing him and beginning the process of forgiveness. *You* are not limited by your brother's stubbornness; it is the possibility of restored relationship that is restricted.

Another limitation to forgiveness is when the offense is ongoing. An alcoholic may become remorseful and loathe himself when he gets sober. He may apologize profusely and swear he'll never get drunk again. But if family members cannot forgive because the same ugly cycle plays itself out week after week, then the limits on forgiveness are not coming from unforgiving hearts; the repeat offender is making it impossible for others to release him, and certainly impossible to have reconciliation.

Yet another limitation to forgiveness is that we can only forgive people who have wronged us; we cannot forgive someone for an offense against someone else. For example, a woman can forgive her husband for abusing her, but she cannot release him for abusing their children. Only the children are in a position to release their father for his offenses.

The Goal: Restoration

In Jeremiah's prophecy about the New Covenant, God says, "I will forgive their wickedness and will remember their sins no more" (31:34). God is not saying that He will erase His awareness of history; He is saying that our sins in the past will not keep us from the future He has planned. God wants us to move into the future with Him in completely restored relationship.

When we are forgiven and when we forgive, love is restored. One day at a Pharisee's house, a woman with a bad moral reputation approached Jesus, crying. Her tears wet His feet and mingled with the expensive perfume she poured over Him. She dried His feet with her hair. Witnesses were offended: *How dare she approach so closely? How dare she show such unrestrained adoration?* But Jesus rebuked them and said, "Her many sins have been forgiven—for she loved much. But he who has been forgiven little loves little" (Luke 7:47).

When we are forgiven and when we forgive, health is restored—health in the life of the individual and health in the life of the Church. Second Chronicles 7:14 says, "If my people, who are called by my name, will humble themselves and pray and seek my face and turn from their wicked ways, then will I hear from heaven and will forgive their sin and will heal their land." The people "who are called by [God's] name," the Church, need to be ready at any time to repent and turn toward God. Then He will forgive and bring healing.

When we are forgiven and when we forgive, relationship is restored. The very last chapter of Genesis is the dramatic conclusion of the story of Joseph, who was betrayed by his brothers, dumped in a pit and sold as a slave. In the years that followed, Joseph was adopted into the culture of the Egyptians and eventually became second-in-command to Pharaoh himself. It was there that he met his brothers again. They came begging the Egyptian court for seed and food in a time of famine.

As the scene unfolds, one finds it easy to expect the sword of justice to fall on the brothers. Instead, their elderly father, Jacob, sends this word to Joseph, so long lost: "I ask you to forgive your brothers the sins and the wrongs they committed in treating you so badly. Now please forgive the sins of the servants of the God of your father." And the passage simply says, "When their message came to him, Joseph wept" (Genesis 50:17).

Joseph forgave. His family was reconciled. And the bloodline of the Messiah continued so that one day the forgiving Rescuer would come to restore us all.

The widow of the man who shot the children in the one-room Amish schoolhouse wrote a letter to the Amish community. Her letter was released to the press just days after the horrific tragedy. Her words are powerful and perhaps unexpected:

> Your love for our family has helped to provide the healing we so desperately need. . . . Your compassion has reached beyond our family, beyond our community, and is changing our world.[2]

Forgiveness is not just what the world needs. Forgiveness is what changes the world.

Notes

1. David Augsburger, *Freedom of Forgiveness* (Chicago, IL: Moody Press, 3rd ed., 2000), p. 9.
2. Marie Roberts, quoted by Stan Roberts, "The Scandal of Forgiveness," *Christianity Today*, January 2007. http://www.christianitytoday.com/ct/2007/january/15.58.html (accessed April 2008).

WEEK 4

DAILY REFLECTIONS

Day 22

Blessed is he whose transgressions are forgiven, whose sins are covered. Blessed is the man whose sin the LORD does not account against him and in whose spirit is no deceit. When I kept silent, my bones wasted away through my groaning all day long . . . Then I acknowledged my sin to you and did not cover up my iniquity. I said, "I will confess my transgressions to the LORD"— and you forgave the guilt of my sin.

PSALM 32:1-5

Have you kept a secret about some dark, embarrassing thing because you know that if it ever came to light, people would look at you differently? You don't want to confess it to another person—and maybe you don't need to—but you can't even imagine confessing it to God. And somewhere deep down, you know that's a mistake.

Know that you are not alone. Those who follow God as closely as can be, such as King David who wrote Psalm 32, are still sinners who remember transgressions of the distant and recent past. David says that when he keeps his sins to himself, when he pretends that he is perfect and doesn't confess to God, the emptiness inside him rots—his bones go soft and brittle.

That's what unconfessed sin does: It eats away at us like a savage disease.

Even when a person gets to the point that he or she wants to confess, there are still doubts and uncertainties: "This is not right and it is not healthy. I am going to come clean and acknowledge to God what He already knows, but what I've never admitted to. But what will happen then? Will God reject me? Will God cast me out of His presence? What will my punishment be?"

Those fears are understandable, but we must never let them keep us from confessing our sin and asking God to forgive us. David says that when he decided to end the covering up, to let his whole life come under the brilliant light of God's truth and righteousness, something wonderful happened: "You forgave the guilt of my sin."

God says that, if we open our eyes and admit our need, He stands ready to release us, to forgive. History cannot be changed, but God can change the future.

Make It Real: Today is as good a time as any to take at least 20 or 30 minutes in a private room or on a walk and confess to God the sins of your past. Take the cover off. Talk to God.

Day 23

Father, forgive them, for they do not know what they are doing.

LUKE 23:34

They had nailed Him to a cross, hoisted the ugly thing in place, watched the blood flow down . . . and then the Roman soldiers heard words from Jesus' lips that must have been hard to believe: "Father, forgive them, for they do not know what they are doing." During His ministry, Jesus had talked about forgiveness continually . . . but in this place? Now?

Imagine you are there. Hear His words, the one word you never expect: *Forgive*. "Curse" seems more appropriate. "Judge" or "condemn" or "destroy." Why should cruel men be forgiven?

Jesus is not calling a wrong a right; He is not morally confused when He offers His forgiveness. But He knows that the Roman soldiers are carrying out their duty of the day as executioners, and they know nothing of the subterfuge behind His betrayal, arrest and mock trial. They don't know this capital punishment is for one not guilty of the crime, or any crime at all.

And so Jesus releases them.

It's important to note that God doesn't forgive *sins*; He forgives *sinners*. We will all, at some point, need forgiveness for things we didn't know we did, for events we caused by accident. Backing the car up, not seeing the kid on the bike, a fluke—and a lifetime of agonizing regret as if there is no such thing as forgiveness.

Some people let themselves off too easily for unintentional mistakes; others torture themselves. The truth that rises above both extremes is that we all need God's loving act of release from transgressions we know we committed *and* for the sins that were unintentional. The Old Testament sacrificial system demonstrated this truth.

In that release, we are truly free.

Make It Real: Talk with God about something you did that hurt someone else, but you did not realize it until later. Ask God to teach you something from the realization and the experience. If appropriate, go to that person and ask for forgiveness.

Day 24

"Lord, how many times should I forgive my brother when he sins against me? Up to seven times?" Jesus answered, "I tell you, not seven times, but seventy times seven."

MATTHEW 18:21-22

Jesus was clear: If we are stingy with forgiveness, everybody suffers.

Jesus followed His comment about "seventy times seven" with a parable about a servant in deep debt to his master, on the verge of bankruptcy and losing his family. The servant was forgiven by his master, who took pity, canceled the debt and let the man go free. But that same servant, who had been forgiven a debt of hundreds of thousands of dollars, then went out and shook down someone who owed him a few days' wages.

This story is just one example of the dozens of ways we are told throughout Scripture: If we receive the blessing of the forgiveness of God, how can we possibly not forgive people we hold in our debt? How can this not be the believer's highest calling, most developed skill and deepest instinct? God forgives us so that we can forgive each other—but this hard-hearted, battle-worn, war-mongering world knows little of the forgiving instinct, and we are often quick to follow its lead rather than God's.

Be honest: What is your gut-level response toward people who are careless with you? If your reaction is to want to get back at those people, you are not alone. But you must ask yourself whether you want to belong to a human race that only knows eye for an eye, tooth for a tooth—or whether you will live in the age of the Messiah, where greater powers allow you to rise above injury and insult.

People who forgive are not saps. They are, in fact, less vulnerable to injury because they refuse to keep their wounds open to bitterness and resentment; they seek healing and restoration as soon as possible. They know that forgiving is not rewarding someone for doing wrong, but releasing that person to a higher court of justice. They know that we all answer to God, so holding moral debts against one another is pointless.

Make It Real: Take a few minutes to think about the most difficult people for you to forgive. Talk to God about why it is so difficult to release them. Figure out the first step toward forgiveness, and take that step.

Day 25

Therefore, as God's chosen people, holy and dearly loved, clothe yourselves with compassion, kindness, humility, gentleness, and patience. Bear with each other and forgive whatever grievances you may have against one another. Forgive as the Lord forgave you. And over all these virtues put on love, which binds them all together in perfect unity.

COLOSSIANS 3:12-14

The bride stands in her pure white, satiny dress and the groom stands beside her, not looking terribly comfortable in his tux. I read these words from Colossians 3 about getting "dressed up," knowing that these three verses give the formula for a healthy marriage: forgiveness clothed in love.

We forgive if we count ourselves among God's people. Why? Because we are "holy" (set apart for God's purposes) and because we are "dearly loved." We are called to a higher plane of existence. The voice of a forgiving God has called us to a new life. He has wrapped His loving arms around us. He has let go of all the insults and acts of disobedience of our entire lives.

How can we be stingy with forgiveness?

As God's chosen people, we wear a certain kind of spiritual "clothing." People see it on the outside, but it comes from the inside. It is not a costume; it is our wardrobe: compassion (the raw instinct of caring), kindness (responding to the needs of others), humility (throwing personal pride to the wind), gentleness (understanding how people operate) and patience (being willing to wait). What an amazing combination! We're all dressed up with everywhere to go!

And to top it off, love "binds [these virtues] all together." We don't have to work hard to squeeze a drop of compassion out of our hearts or do a lot of research about the history and methods of kindness. We want to be humble. We long to be patient. And we want to forgive. It all boils down to motivation. If love is our highest motive, as Jesus said it must be, then gentleness, forgiveness and the other virtues flow freely.

Make It Real: Write down these words on a piece of paper and carry them in your pocket today: *compassion*, *kindness*, *humility*, *gentleness* and *patience*. Repeat them to yourself when you find yourself in a trying situation, whether it's a traffic jam, a frustrating co-worker or kids who are driving you nuts!

Day 26

If we claim to be without sin, we deceive ourselves and the truth is not in us. If we confess our sins, he is faithful and just and will forgive us our sins and purify us from all unrighteousness.

1 JOHN 1:8-9

She was a well-known novelist and secular humanist, but in a television interview in 1988, shortly before she died, Marghanita Laski made a surprising admission: "What I envy most about you Christians is your forgiveness; I have nobody to forgive me."[1] What an awful thing—to feel that you need to be forgiven, that you are responsible to some higher authority, but to disbelieve that there is any God who can help you. That there is no one to grant absolution.

In the church where I grew up, there came a time in the worship services when the pastor made a pronouncement of absolution, which is a formal declaration of being released from guilt, penalty and obligation. When words like that rang out loud and clear, many of us felt the ground become solid under our feet. We knew we were forgiven.

If absolution stopped with a church leader declaring forgiveness, doubts might linger. But we have the bold declarations of God's Word to bring absolution with confidence: "Though your sins are like scarlet they will be white as snow" (Isaiah 1:18); "As far as the east is from the west, so far has God removed our transgressions from us" (Psalm 103:12).

Words of absolution come after confession, but it is not the voicing of confession that makes forgiveness happen, nor even the mental recollection of our misdeeds. If that were the case, then we would likely live in anxiety, worrying that we may have forgotten something or hadn't confessed convincingly enough.

No, forgiveness comes because God "is faithful and just," and because He chooses to extend mercy and grace. And when He forgives, God intends to move us in the right direction. He purifies us "from all unrighteousness." God doesn't merely want to get the thief to stop stealing; He wants to transform the thief's heart from greed to generosity. It is good when the cantankerous person stops insulting and demeaning others, but God wants more: to transform his or her heart.

Make It Real: Think about someone you know who needs a reminder that God has forgiven him or her, an "absolution." Either pray for that person or seek a way to remind him or her through a note or in person.

Day 27

And the teachers of the law who came down from Jerusalem said, "He is possessed by Beelzebub! By the prince of demons he is driving out demons" . . . "I tell you the truth, all the sins and blasphemies of men will be forgiven them. But who ever blasphemes against the Holy Spirit will never be forgiven; he is guilty of an eternal sin."

MARK 3:22,28-29

Zacarias Moussaoui was defiant to the end of his trial. It is a known fact that he had taken flying lessons with the terrorists who attacked on 9/11, preparing himself for the most unthinkable and heinous act. He was proud of it. In his closing arguments, prosecutor David Raskin said that Moussaoui's own testimony demonstrated that he had no remorse and personified "unforgivable evil."[2] Raskin was right, but not perhaps for the right reason. There *is* sin that is unforgivable, but it is unforgivable not because of its *degree* but because it is ongoing and remorseless.

Jesus made His statement about the unpardonable sin one day when He was in conflict with a group of religious people, the teachers of the law. It was a low point in His ministry. Jesus had been healing people and casting out demons—the most spectacular display of God's awesome power—and then the teachers of the law called Jesus possessed, claiming that the spirit by which He drove out demons was the spirit of Satan himself.

They turned all of reality upside down. These teachers of the law were not just blind to the amazing work of the Holy Spirit in their midst; they were calling the work of the Holy Spirit the work of the devil! To call God's work the work of Satan is to decide completely and absolutely not to believe, and this is the unpardonable sin.

For believers with a tender conscience who worry that in a phase of doubt they have committed the unpardonable sin, be assured: It is only when someone refuses to believe and continues in that condition, unwilling to fall on the mercy of Christ, that the guilt of sin hangs over their head.

Make It Real: Think of someone who refuses to believe in God, and spend some time interceding on their behalf. Get on your knees and pray that God will give you an opportunity to show them His transforming love today.

Day 28

For I will forgive their wickedness and will remember their sins no more.

JEREMIAH 31:34

It happened again, as it had so many times before: The stepfather got so frustrated and angry at his stepdaughter that he blew his top. She wasn't complying with his standards, and he was frustrated that his wife would not clamp down on her more. So he got heated. He got agitated. All of a sudden, he was shouting, pacing, shaking his fist and calling her demeaning names. Thirty minutes later, when no one was talking to anyone else, he slipped into remorse and asked for forgiveness—but was miffed when that forgiveness was not handed to him on a silver platter. "What happened to love?" he asked. "What happened to 'forgive and forget'?"

We've all heard the expression "forgive and forget," often from people who have done wrong and would like the whole world to pretend it never happened. Or it comes from people who would rather gloss over something that someone else did rather than tell them how hurtful it was.

It is true that God says, "I will remember their sins no more," but what does that mean exactly? Can God choose to have a memory lapse? Does God reach backward and change history? Does He want us to think that we have the power to change history?

If that were the case, the Bible wouldn't be so full of history. It is, in fact, a vivid account of the accomplishments and the failures of God's people.

The smaller offences can be forgotten more easily, but the most devastating events that happen in our lives become part of our personal histories. Throughout our lives, we will recollect them from time to time—and that is good, because we will continue to learn from them. History is history, and it can't be rewritten . . . but it can be a teacher, if we will allow it.

Forgive and forget is possible in this way: Offenses go from being in the forefront of our thinking (sometimes even to the point of obsession) to the background of our minds. The hurts get filed farther and farther back in the filing cabinet until finally, one day in the distant future, all that is left is peace and restoration. As 1 Corinthians 13, the "love chapter," puts it: "[Love] keeps no record of wrongs" (v. 5).

Make It Real: On a piece of paper, write down two different incidents when someone has hurt you badly. Then ask yourself whether you've released those situations into the hands of God and His justice. Write on the back side of the paper "Love keeps no record of wrongs," then tear it up into the smallest pieces you can and throw them away.

Notes

1. Quoted by John Stott, "The Contemporary Christian," *Christianity Today*, Vol. 38, no. 7.
2. Quoted by Phil Hischkorn, "Jury Deliberations Begin in 9/11 Trial," CNN.com, April 26, 2006. http://edition.cnn.com/2006/LAW/04/24/moussaoui.trial/index.html (accessed April 2008).

WEEK 4

GROUP DISCUSSION QUESTIONS

1. What has "forgiveness" meant to you in the past? How does that line up with what was said in this chapter and how is it different?

2. What mistaken ideas about forgiveness have you run into in other people?

3. What is hard about releasing someone? Are there reasons we might want to hold on to resentment?

4. How can you tell people you forgive them (that is, release them from debt to you) without endorsing their misbehavior?

5. What can you do with people who continually ask forgiveness for the exact same wrongs?

6. What does being forgiven by God in Christ mean to you personally?

7. How can you let the grace, love and forgiveness of Christ shape your attitudes?

8. Do you have problems with the idea that God forgives people that you have real problems with?

WEEK 5

HEALING

Letting God Restore Your Spirit, Your Body and Your Relationships

In the earliest days of Jesus' ministry, rumor spread that He was miraculously healing people who had physical and other ailments. Even so, the people in Nazareth's synagogue on the day Jesus announced Jubilee, the acceptable year of the Lord, must have been stunned to hear Him say that He had been sent to "proclaim recovery of sight for the blind" (Luke 4:18).

Blindness has a spiritual meaning—Christ opens our spiritual vision so that we can see God—but there were times when Jesus used divine power to show that God can literally reverse disease and disability. He didn't heal everybody then, just as He doesn't heal everyone today, but He healed enough people to make it clear that when He remakes heaven and earth one day, He will banish injury and sickness forever. His announcement of "recovery of slight for the blind" was the first installment of recovery for the world.

Throughout the Old Testament, we find promises of healing and prophesies about a healer who would come to signal God's power and work. Those promises were kept and the prophecies fulfilled in the coming of Jesus, who healed people as a sign of God's continuing and future work in the world. God's activity *includes* healing but is much, much more. This is important, because there are plenty of people who have been taken in by "faith healers" and been left hurt or terribly confused. Instead of receiving healing, they have gotten nothing but hopelessness. If you have ever been confused by someone's claim to have the power of healing–if it just didn't seem quite right or sounded weird and imbalanced–it is quite possible that they detached "healing" from the wider work of God. We can only understand God's healing work when we begin to understand the whole of God's work. Healing (whether physical, emotional, spiritual or relational) is deeply connected to God's other Jubilee work in our lives (redemption, freedom, forgiveness, and so on). Detach healing from these truths, and we end up with a distorted view of healing that expects either too little or too much.

We need healing–whole, Jubilee healing–in every sense of the word. We need physical healing, emotional healing, spiritual healing and relational healing, both with God and with others. Recovery of sight for the blind is the sign we've all been waiting for.

The Healing of the Land in Jubilee

Believers sometimes quote 2 Chronicles 7:14 to express their longing for the healing of their home nation:

> If my people, who are called by my name, will humble themselves and pray and seek my face and turn from their wicked ways, then will I hear from heaven and will forgive their sin and will *heal their land* (emphasis added).

We should not be surprised that this passage prompts us to think about the nations where we live; is there any doubt that your country is in need of healing? But because this promise was given to the Hebrew people in the Old Testament era, it is most precisely applied in our day to the Church rather than the country in which we reside. "My people . . . called by my name" does not refer to a particular nation, but to the people of God. And as His people, we need to humble ourselves, pray, seek Him and turn from any wickedness—then God will hear, forgive and heal us.

In the verse above, as well as in Leviticus 25 (the "Jubilee passage") and other places where God makes a promise about "the land," it's important to know that people in ancient times understood these words *literally*. In the Jubilee passage, God told the people that during the special Sabbath year, they should not plant their crops (vv. 4-5). They should take a *Shabbat*, a rest, for themselves and they should also give the land a rest. In modern times, agricultural science has demonstrated how repeated and relentless use of the land can exhaust it; land can get depleted and bruised, and it needs rest and recovery. God was way ahead of modern science. He commanded His children to give their land a rest.

What was good for the land was good for the people, who gained a rhythm of work and rest. Sabbath. As they allowed their land to lie fallow and heal, they also experienced God's healing.

Seeking the Healing Power of God

I know plenty of people who are hardly ever sick, and I know people who deal with illness, disease and chronic disabilities over the course of years. I have also known extraordinarily healthy people who were able to say, "I've never been sick a day in my life" . . . until one day when the blood test came back positive, when the X-ray showed a shadow or when the headaches began.

No matter our personal experience with health and sickness, we can know that the mission of the Messiah includes healing. Living a healthy life (insofar as doing so is within our power) and seeking spiritual and physical healing is a normal part of the Christian life. Taking health seriously honors God.

As I have talked to various groups about Jubilee and its interwoven themes, I have been struck by how surprising the ideas are for many people. It seems to me that many of us have read the Bible for years but have never connected the dots between these concepts. Many people are surprised to discover that God has specific ways in which He brings healing: through Sabbath, forgiveness, freedom and the other works of God in Jubilee.

Yet even when the big picture of healing and Jubilee begins to become clear, they have questions. They wonder, *Does God still do miracles? Does He heal us physically as well as spiritually? Is it okay to pray for physical healing, or should we only pray a confession of our sins? Or both?*

In the epistle of James in the New Testament, we get some answers.

> Is any one of you in trouble? He should pray. Is anyone happy? Let him sing songs of praise. Is any one of you sick? He should call the elders of the church to pray over him and anoint him with oil in the name of the Lord. And the prayer offered in faith will make the sick person well; the Lord will raise him up. If he has sinned,

> he will be forgiven. Therefore confess your sins to each other and pray for each other so that you may be healed. The prayer of a righteous man is powerful and effective (James 5:13-16).

I love that this passage covers all the days of our lives. Days of trouble and days of happiness. Days of illness and days of health. Days when we live in the freedom of forgiveness and days when there is sin we leave unconfessed.

Let's look at these verses in detail.

First, James says that we should seek God in times of trouble and in times of contentment (see v. 13). The word translated here as "trouble" refers to any kind of distress. You name it: times when you're in mourning because you've lost a loved one, when you're in terrible conflict, when things are difficult at work or at home—if you're in trouble of any kind, James says: *Pray!*

If that sounds cliché, keep in mind that James's letter is not an epistle of easy answers. James means serious business when he says that the person in trouble should pray, and for very good reasons. Distress tends to cause us to isolate ourselves—to roll up in a ball and become passive when trouble roars. Prayer, on the other hand, opens us to God in His greatness. It is our lifeline to Him. It focuses our eyes on the face of Jesus and connects us to the Holy Spirit, who is always among us, always working.

Are you in trouble today? Go to a quiet place, take a walk or call a friend . . . and reach out to God in prayer.

The same thing applies if this is a day of happiness, James says. Wise people connect with God in prayer on days when they are content and things are going well, because they know that prayer shapes us–it opens us to the mind and heart of God. If we only pray when we are distressed, our conversations with God are always associated with what is not right in the world and in our lives. We need to pray during good days to understand the way things are supposed to be and to form a healthy picture of God and who He created us to be.

Next, James says that if you are ill, you should seek God in prayer (see v. 14). Many people, even in the modern era, testify to the wisdom of James's advice: Dale Matthew of Georgetown University estimates that about 75 percent of studies on spirituality have confirmed that prayer has health benefits. "If prayer were available in pill form, no pharmacy could stock enough of it."[1]

Before we get too far, let's agree that there are different kinds of illnesses: body, mind and spirit. The Hebrew mindset sees a person as a whole being–physical, mental, emotional and spiritual sicknesses are all potent realities that negatively affect a person's wholeness. This understanding is quite a contrast from modern believers who acknowledge physical and spiritual illness but ignore mental and emotional disorders. Is it because they consider the mind to be a special spiritual territory that has not been affected by the damage the Fall? The human race has become ill in every way. There is no part of our lives that is not touched by the sickness of sin, so there is no part of us that does not need healing.

James says that prayer for healing is both a personal prayer and a call for other mature people to pray on our behalf. We can and should always pray to God about our own physical limitations, but we should enlist the prayer support of others when the burden of illness or injury is particularly heavy. When James mentioned the prayer of elders, he was *not* intending to limit effective intercessory prayer to "officials" in the Church; it is not only the governing board of a local church or ordained clergy who are empowered to pray for healing. The word "elder" in the Early Church (as in Jewish synagogues at the time) referred to the especially mature believers within the worshiping community who were considered stable and wise. Many of the house churches at that time had a few dozen members. The "elders" of these communities were the clearly recognized spiritual pillars. Today, as then, it is the spiritually mature, scattered throughout the global Church, who stand ready to pray what James calls "the prayer of faith."

Verse 14 mentions anointing with oil. What is that all about? There are two different ways of understanding anointing and probably both apply. First, putting a dab of oil on a person's head was, in Old Testament times, a symbol of God's blessing and presence. Second, the oil derived from olives in Israel was a primary medicine in a day and age that had nothing like the pharmaceuticals we have today. (In the parable of the Good Samaritan, the Samaritan applies wine and oil to the wounds of the beaten man to clean and soothe them.)

So when James talks about anointing the sick person with oil, he is painting a picture of using both prayer and medical treatment as instruments of healing. It is a shame when people think only doctors and medicines heal. And it is a tragedy when some believe that only prayer is needed and ignore the skilled gifts of medical professionals. (For example, in the early 1970s a man named Larry Parker and his wife, who belonged to a church that believed healing always occurs with enough faith, withheld insulin from their diabetic son, Wesley. Predictably, Wesley went into a diabetic coma and subsequently died. Larry and his wife were convicted of manslaughter and child abuse.[2])

What is this "prayer offered in faith" mentioned in verse 15 that makes the sick person whole? Everybody wants healing; nobody wants to wait for healing that will come only after the return of Christ in the New Creation. Because of this pervasive longing, some have taught a terrible principle about the "prayer of faith" that has done much damage: *Healing is guaranteed to anybody as long as he or she has enough faith.* I have known people who have been told that the reason they have not been healed is that their prayers have not been strong enough or long enough, or that their prayers lacked faith.

That is just wrong. So wrong. From the oldest book in the Old Testament, Job, all the way through to Revelation, we are taught that we live in a broken world that includes germs and cancer cells, famines and earthquakes. God will one day fix the whole world, and there are many repairs He makes in the meantime to the brokenness around us. But healing is *His* prerogative, not ours; no one—through faith or anything else—is given absolute power to determine who will get better.

The "prayer of faith" is not faith in prayer or faith in oil or faith in people who are praying for you, but faith in God. Praying the prayer of faith is an act of totally resigning oneself to God's care (and sometimes illness or injury is what finally prompts us to say words like these to God):

> Dear Lord, I am hurting. I understand today more than on other days that I am a creature made of dust. I realize

now that I have taken healthy days for granted. Lord, I need You. Please take care of my ailing body. Please bring a restoring touch. If my actions or neglect have brought on my illness, I am willing to learn from my mistakes. I know You are powerful and good. Thank You for medical resources, but I know I need more. I need You. I entrust myself to You. I lay myself in Your care. Give me faith and courage to face whatever lies ahead.

In the Christian life, we come to God in prayer—carrying all our diseases and disabilities, our guilt and innocence—and lay ourselves before Him, trusting in His grace. That's the plain and simple meaning of "the prayer of faith": throwing yourself on the mercy of God, falling into God's embrace and moving into an uncertain tomorrow—not because you are in control of your destiny, but because you know that God knows your destiny.

This is where things might begin to get tricky. James says next that "prayer offered in faith will make the sick person well" and that "the Lord will raise him up" (v. 15). Don't these sound like guarantees?

Whatever they are, they can't be guarantees—since James's day, the strongest believers who have lived the most faithful lives have all succumbed to death. No human being has ever fended off all disease, injury and death through his or her great faith. So why would James say so? Because *generally* it is true. We pray for people who are ill, and most of the time they get well. People have prayed for me when I needed physical healing more times than I can count: when I had a throat infection and had to go to a speaking engagement, when I had a virus that held on for weeks, when I broke a rib water-skiing, when I flew over the handle bars of my bike onto the pavement and sustained a significant head injury and broken bones. (My brain didn't work right for weeks after that accident. People heard me talk in my altered state and were motivated to pray! I learned later that many people received phone calls and started praying even as I was loaded into an ambulance.)

Each time, when people have prayed, I have been healed.

Now some will say, "Wait a minute . . . that's just natural healing! It's not *real* healing, as in supernatural, throw-your-cane-away, open-your-eyes, walk-for-the-first-time healing."

And my response is, "What do you mean, *just* natural healing? Do you attribute to God only the out-of-the-ordinary kinds of healing, and not *every* kind of healing? Who gets credit for all the healing that has already occurred in your life? Did you heal your leg when you broke it as a kid? Were you the one to suppress that infection you had last year? Was it some 'natural' force that healed your abdomen after the surgeon removed your gall bladder?"

We make a mistake when we make too bold a distinction between the natural and the supernatural.

When I broke my clavicle and the orthopedic doctor told me there was nothing he could do about it, that it had to just "heal on its own," it *did* heal. That's amazing! I broke my face and bruised my brain, but they healed. Months later, the doctor showed me the knot-like shape where bone tissue had developed between and over the fracture on my clavicle, and I knew he was wrong. It didn't just "heal on its own." That may have been natural healing, but it seemed super to me.

God heals. He heals physically and in every other way. Does He heal every time? No. Though I have been healed dozens of times, there may come a day when I develop a malady for which there is no healing, and that will be my opportunity to cross from this life to the life to come, where healing is permanent.

The book of James in the New Testament is a lot like the book of Proverbs in the Old Testament. Both give practical wisdom and life perspectives that explain to us the way things happen *generally*, though not in every single instance. Think about it: We get sick many, many times in our lives, and we are healed many, many times. How many times is a typical person healed in an average lifespan? Dozens? Hundreds? Thousands? We can never know. None of us knows how many attacks by microbes and rebellious cells are being put down by the amazing healing and regenerative power that God has put in our bodies. We don't know how many times something potentially lethal has attacked us.

What James says about the sick being healed and raised up is true, *generally*. If you're sick, pray. Ask others to pray for you. You will be restored, *generally* speaking.

In other words, God is "making us whole" all the time. But not every time. And that is where the struggle comes in.

Sometimes believers wrestle with whether or not it is okay to ask God for healing. *What if this is the time when healing will not come? What if this is the last disease?* Thankfully, none of us knows when our last day will come. Neither do we need to pretend as if we can predict what tomorrow will bring. We must not pretend that we know more than we do. Faith means moving ahead in life even though we do not know the future.

Is it okay to ask God for healing? Of course! We don't need to predict the likely outcome of our situation to decide whether or not to ask for healing prayer. Our heavenly Father never sees a request for healing as improper. Maybe the sick person will receive physical healing and maybe not, but even then—I can tell you from having seen it many times over—hurting people are "raised up." Even when a disease is not suppressed, the person's spirit is raised up by God's own Spirit and the loving attention of others, and is able to proceed day by day with a greater sense of peace.

What about sickness and confession of sin, mentioned in verses 15 and 16? The Bible does teach that sometimes there is a connection between our illness and sin. We see this dynamic most obviously in cases when an ailment is a consequence of poor choices: One person contracts a sexually transmitted disease because he or she is living a life of promiscuity; another person develops lung cancer after a lifetime of smoking; someone else's liver begins to shut down after years of alcohol abuse; a teenager drives a car that is full of her friends off the road at 2:00 A.M. and hits a tree because they were all under the influence of alcohol. Sin and consequence. Risk and injury.

The statistics of preventable diseases are staggering. Just think what would happen to our healthcare crisis if we lived according to the character of Christ. The percentages of people with lung cancer, cirrhosis of the liver and high blood pressure would drop dramatically. The death rate of teenagers would be a fraction of what it is today. Our choices in lifestyle often lead directly to health or illness, life or death.

Having said all that, there are many ailments that are not linked at all with reckless or injudicious behavior. High cholesterol that led to a heart attack may just be genes. Rheumatoid arthritis set in, but nothing could have prevented it. A baby is born with a heart defect. Someone ends up in traction not because he drove his car recklessly, but because the other guy ran a light and broadsided him. Almost always, these kinds of injuries and illnesses have nothing to do with sin in our lives, and we should never make the assumption that our distress is God's punishment.

The Bible prescribes one thing for dealing with painful sicknesses and hurts: the prayers of righteous men and women (see v. 16). When His righteous people pray, God may work through the natural regenerative process of the body or He may work supernaturally to intensify or speed up the natural process. He may give us the strength to be revived in our spirits to go on to the next day with dignity, or He may allow this disease or injury to be our very last. In whatever way He chooses to heal us, it is the effective and powerful prayers of godly men and women that invite His mercy and healing grace.

Preparing for Trouble and Illness

The following are four ways that we can prepare for trouble and illness that may inflict our lives.

1. Keep the Prayer Connection with God Strong

We are most prepared from trouble when we are diligent during good times about staying connected with God through prayer. Prayer, whether offered in trouble or health, gives us hope. A medical study of 122 men who had their first heart attack found that, of the 25 most pessimistic men, 21 had died eight years later. Of the 25 most optimistic, only 6 had died.[3] Hope, in other words, is a greater predictor of survival than other medical factors. Our hope is strengthened as we spend time with God in prayer.

2. Enjoy Health, but Do Not Be Surprised by Illness

Enjoy health when you've got it, but don't be surprised when your body shows itself to be vulnerable and changeable. The Bible says that "we have this treasure in jars of clay" (2 Corinthians 4:7). It also says that when we suffer, the Christ who is available to come along side us is a sufferer, too. Philippians 3 talks about the fellowship of sharing in His sufferings. We should not be shocked when suffering comes.

3. Ask for the Prayer Support of Others

Don't be shy. Don't hold back. Be engaged with the people of God in a small group or some other setting. It is best if you can ask for prayer from people who know you well, but if that is not a possibility right now, ask for prayer anyway.

4. Be an Agent of Healing

If you pray for someone else, you are a healer. If you call someone or email someone who is housebound by their illness, you are an agent of healing. If you know someone who is in a dire, life-threatening situation and you organize some people to pray, you are a healer. If you visit a friend in the hospital, you are a healer.

Bring a smile with you. Bring a magazine, a gift. Bring a listening ear. Bring faith, love and hope. Bring good humor. (Last October, I visited someone in the hospital who had hip replacement surgery. As I talked with her, she told me that her friends had played a rather novel joke on her. While she was under general anesthesia for several hours, they decorated her room with Christmas decorations. As she was slowly emerging from her anesthesia, they told her that she had been in a coma for two months and had just woken up. With friends like that . . .)

Focus on the Healer

I want to close this chapter by telling you about a man I've had the privilege of getting to know in recent years. Ed Dobson was pastor of Calvary Church in Grand Rapids, Michigan, for over 20 years. Several years ago he was diagnosed with ALS, Lou Gehrig's disease. At first he hoped he would have the mildest form of ALS–wherein the nerve damage and atrophied muscles are limited to one hand and arm–but he knew that the diagnosis was not good, and that it was likely he would finally succumb to the disease.

Ed prayed in every way possible. When his faith was small, he prayed, "Lord, I'll give up my right hand; just let the disease stop there." If he was a little stronger in his faith, he prayed, "Lord, stop it right where it is; let it get no worse than it is today." If he was feeling particularly bold, he prayed, "Maybe You could heal me, Lord. Maybe You could reverse this disease."

While in Israel, Ed went to the Wailing Wall and had one of the rabbis there pray for him. He had gotten to the point where his theology of the day was, "I'll try anything if it might work."

But the disease continued to progress.

One night, he asked a fellow pastor in Grand Rapids to come over and pray a healing prayer for him. When the pastor came, he told Ed stories about people who had been physically healed and stories about some who had not been. And then the pastor said this: "Ed, you need to get lost in the wonder of God. If you get lost in that wonder, who knows what He'll do for you?"

Ed is retired now, and the ALS has not regressed. It could very well be that this disease will be Ed's last. But he says that of all the advice he has gotten from a multitude of people, nothing comes close to "get lost in the wonder of God." He has refocused on the Healer, rather than the healing, and that has made all the difference in the world.

That's the way I want to be if and when I get very ill.

Notes

1. Dianne Hales, "Why Prayer Could Be Good Medicine," *Parade Magazine*, March 2003.
2. Larry Parker, *We Let Our Son Die* (Eugene, OR: Harvest House Publishers, 1980). See also Hank Hanegraaff, *Christianity in Crisis* (Eugene, OR: Harvest House Publishers, 1997).
3. Daniel Goleman, "Doctors Find Comfort Is a Potent Medicine," *New York Times*, November 26, 1991.

WEEK 5

DAILY REFLECTIONS

Day 29

He has sent me to proclaim . . . recovery of sight for the blind.

LUKE 4:18

He was the last person in the world to think he would ever get better. The man, blind from birth, had lived a life of total darkness. He had never known anything different.

He sat hour after hour on the hard pavement of Jerusalem streets, his beggar's hand extended, hoping for a few coins to make it through the day. And then one day, he heard a group of people talking about him as if he wasn't there.

The first voice asked rudely, "Who sinned, this man or his parents, that he was born blind?"

The answer from the second voice was stunning: "Neither. This happened so that the work of God might be displayed in his life. While I am in the world, I am the light of the world."

Then the blind man heard someone spit in the dirt, felt mud spread on his eyes and heard the second voice tell him to go and wash in the pool of Siloam. He groped his way through narrow streets across town to the ritual pool. With the application of water, something happened for the first time in is life: He could see.

John 9 goes on to tell about the Pharisees interrogating the formerly blind man and objecting that the healing had taken place on the Sabbath. In response, Jesus told them that they were the ones who were truly blind.

On J-Day, when He read from the scroll of Isaiah in the synagogue in Nazareth, Jesus proclaimed recovery of sight for the blind. The Year of Jubilee, "the acceptable year of the Lord," would include miraculous healings: disabled people walking, deaf people hearing, blind people seeing. Although Jesus didn't heal everybody, He healed enough people to make the sign bold and clear: *The power of God has come into the world and now everything will be different.*

Once in a great while, something as miraculous as a blind person regaining sight happens—and each time is a promise that one day, when God remakes heaven and earth, each of us will see clearly for the first time. The Messiah was sent to proclaim "recovery of sight for the blind." Lord, let us see what we need to see today.

Make It Real: Make a commitment to contact a church or a community agency that helps those who struggle with physical, mental or emotional health. Volunteer to serve a meal, visit a senior center or simply sit and talk with those who are hurting.

Day 30

Peace I leave with you; my peace I give you. I do not give to you as the world gives. Do not let your hearts be troubled and do not be afraid.

JOHN 14:27

You're walking down the sidewalk and see a longtime acquaintance. If there is no time to stop and talk, you nod and simply say "Hi" or "How ya doin'?" Maybe you mean it, or maybe the words are just words.

The Hebrews had a much better way of greeting each other: "*Shalom.*" The usual translation into English is "peace," and though this translation isn't wrong, it is lacking. Shalom is a weighty word that expresses full, complete blessing. Shalom is not just the absence of conflict, but a total wholeness of being. When someone greets another with "Shalom," it doesn't just mean, "Hi, hope you have a good day." It implies, "May you enjoy security and safety, may you experience harmony and accord in all parts of your life, and may you have soundness, completeness and health in every respect." Shalom means health. It points to how we are healed.

Jesus greeted His disciples many times with the word "Shalom." And they most certainly never forgot that day after Jesus' death and resurrection when He suddenly appeared in the room with them and said, "Shalom" (see Luke 24:36). Shalom, indeed! The risen Messiah is our greatest hope for complete healing.

How do we heal? We are, in fact, being healed all the time. When we are cut or bruised, our bodies have an amazing capacity to heal themselves. Likewise, our bodies are continually attacked by microbes and germs that are unseen, and by God's design, we are defended.

But the most important healing happens to the wholeness of our being when Christ brings peace to our troubled soul or fearful heart, when He rejoins us in fellowship with the heavenly Father, and when He breaks apart flaws in our character, such as pride and resentment. This is true healing.

Make It Real: Find a peaceful place today—maybe a park, a quiet room, a nature trail or a library—and pray for God's peace in a troubling situation in your life.

Day 31

If it is possible, as far as it depends on you, live at peace with everyone.

ROMANS 12:18

Elizabeth Barrett married Robert Browning in 1846 in secret because of her certainty that her tyrannical father would disapprove. He did. The couple sailed to Italy, where they lived the rest of their lives, but Elizabeth kept trying to reach out to her parents by writing a letter every week over 10 years—even though she never got a single one in reply. After 10 years, Elizabeth received a large box from the U.S. that contained her letters to her parents. All of them. Unopened.

Those same letters were later published and are regarded as a treasure in English literature. If only her parents had listened. If only reconciliation could have happened.

One reason to believe in healing is so that we don't miss an opportunity to experience it. The healing of reconciliation, for instance, may only be one letter away.

Many people experience healing in their lives when they are in their last days. At the eleventh hour, they have the opportunity to take stock of their lives. This is the time when many people say things that should have been said—*could* have been said—long ago: "I'm sorry." "I'm proud of you." "You have helped me." "I appreciate what you did." "I love you." Saying what should be said brings healing. It's never too late to try to make amends.

It's too bad that sometimes it takes being in the final stage of life to shake us free from all the frivolous, superficial distractions of life so that we can finally get down to really living. Sometimes we notice the glory of the sun only when it is about to set.

Yet the fact that there can be healing even at that time should tell us that healing is always possible. We don't have complete control over our relationships, but we can follow what Romans 12:18 says: "If it is possible, as far as it depends on you, live at peace with everyone." We can't control all the circumstances of our lives, but we can make choices about what our attitudes will be toward our circumstances.

Make It Real: Prayerfully consider someone with whom you need to be reconciled. Ask the Lord to bring healing to your heart so that you can access the power of forgiveness, which is what makes reconciliation possible. Consider writing that person a letter to bridge the gap between you.

Day 32

Is any one of you sick? He should call the elders of the church to pray over him and anoint him with oil in the name of the Lord. And the prayer offered in faith will make the sick person well; the Lord will raise him up. If he has sinned, he will be forgiven.

JAMES 5:14-15

Does physical healing actually occur? Does it make sense to pray for physical healing? For minor illnesses? For terminal conditions? The simple answer to these questions is *yes*. The Bible says that any child of God may come to Him at any time, asking for what seems to be good.

We know that we live in a world of health and illness. We have bodies that function well sometimes, but often get sick and someday will die. We also know that we recover from illnesses all the time and that the body is healing itself in ways we aren't even aware of. Who can know how many times a person in an average lifespan is healed from vicious viruses or malignant cells? A thousand times? Ten thousand times? None of us knows for sure. God's healing work is going on invisibly all the time. God's healing power working through protective white blood cells is the same power through which Jesus healed blind people–one is just more typical than the other. "Supernatural" in comparison with "natural" is just a matter of frequency. God is Lord of both realms.

So when James says in his epistle that when we are seriously ill we should have people pray for us, we are simply entrusting ourselves to God. We do this knowing that there are many natural healing processes that go on (including medical treatment) and that supernatural healing is always a possibility. There is no better thing for us to do whenever distress happens in life than to place ourselves in the care of the God who created us and loves us. That's what "the prayer of faith" means; it is not a prayer to demand healing, but a prayer that entrusts ourselves to God.

The "prayer of faith" will generally make the sick person well. James's words in the New Testament are like the Proverbs in the Old Testament: They both say what *typically* happens. We are healed from most attacks on our bodies in our lifetimes. Yet whether we are physically healed or not, we can look to God to "raise us up"—to have hope where others would be hopeless.

Make It Real: Make a list of the ways you have needed physical healing in your life, whether illness or injury. Reflect on the list and take a few minutes to praise God for how He has held you up. Then pray for ways you need healing today.

Day 33

If he has sinned, he will be forgiven.

JAMES 5:15

We know that sickness is a real issue in life and we know that we need our sin to be forgiven—but is there a relationship between the two?

On the one hand, we know that it is very unhelpful—even damaging or devastating—when a seriously ill person keeps asking, "What have I done wrong? Where have I sinned? Why is God punishing me?" We know from the book of Job that this is not the right way to think about calamities in our lives. Job was the man who suffered almost more than can be imagined and was told by his "friends" that his serious condition must mean that he did something terribly wrong, that he had failed God in a major way. Why else would God be putting him through this?

Occasionally we do get sick because our sin causes the sickness—our illness is a direct consequence. If you choose to abuse drugs or to be sexually promiscuous, you may suffer the consequences of addiction or a sexually transmitted disease. (In 1 Corinthians 10, the apostle Paul says that some in that Church were getting ill because of their severe spiritual disobedience.) On the other hand, sometimes we are ill just because we live in a world of viruses and carcinogens and earthquakes. Job was a sinner and he lived in a world of fellow sinners, a world that is broken and often sick because of sin.

The bottom line is this: When we are ill we should ask, *Did I do something that obviously caused this?* And if there is no obvious answer, we should not assume God is punishing us and not telling us why.

So what about "If he has sinned, he will be forgiven"? James means that when we are in distress and pray "the prayer of faith," truly entrusting ourselves to God, we will know God's forgiveness and He will "raise us up." It all works together—spiritual health, physical health.

Make It Real: List three aspects of your lifestyle that you know affect your health in a negative way. Make a pledge to change at least one of these things beginning this week.

Day 34

For six years sow your fields, and for six years prune your vineyards and gather their crops. But in the seventh year the land is to have a Sabbath of rest, a Sabbath to the LORD. Do not sow your fields or prune your vineyards. Do not reap what grows of itself or harvest the grapes of your untended vines. The land is to have a year of rest.

LEVITICUS 25:3-5

George Washington Carver (1864-1943) is often remembered as the peanut farmer who invented peanut butter. (And where would the world be without peanut butter?) But Carver was much more. He became an expert agriculturalist and led a revolution of farming methods in the South, where fields were exhausted by cotton. He introduced sustainable farming practices that gave the land rest and replenishment, such as crop rotation and planting protein-rich crops like soy and sweet potatoes.

Even land needs healing. Pressed to exhaustion, land is of no use to anybody, becoming a wasteland. That is why the Year of Jubilee described in Leviticus 25 was a time for the Israelites to let the land lie fallow (that is, not plant crops) and allow the soil to regain its nutrients and moisture.

Jubilee was freedom for the slave, redemption from bondage and healing for the land and people. George Washington Carver, a remarkable inventor and entrepreneur who embodied these themes, was born a slave. When only an infant, he and his mother were abducted by slave raiders. His mother was sold and shipped away, but George's master bought him back from the raiders in exchange for a horse. Carver eventually went to high school and became the first black student at Simpson College.

He earned a masters' degree in agriculture and became a professor. Slavery, redemption, healing.

Jubilee brings so many of the needs of our lives together: healing, redemption, freedom. When we rest and remind ourselves that only God is God, then He brings healing, restoration and life.

Make It Real: Today, eliminate one thing you normally try to squeeze into your schedule. Take that time to rest or relax with a walk. Be still and focus on the fact that only God is God.

Day 35

Therefore, to keep me from becoming conceited, there was given me a thorn in my flesh, a messenger of Satan, to torment me. Three times I pleaded with the Lord to take it away from me. But he said to me, "My grace is sufficient for you, for my power is made perfect in weakness." Therefore I will boast all the more gladly about my weaknesses, so that Christ's power may rest on me.

2 CORINTHIANS 12:7-9

In a film about a man coming to terms with his wife's progressive Alzheimer's disease, the husband one day loses his cool. He shakes her by the shoulders and screams, "I hate you, Iris, you stupid cow! I loathe you, every inch of you! . . . I've got you now, and I don't want you!"

Contrast that with Roberston McQuilken, who for 20 years was president of Columbia Bible College and was a world-recognized Christian leader. He resigned his position in order to care for his wife, who had advanced Alzheimer's (the full story is told in the book *A Promise Kept*). In his letter of resignation, McQuilken explained that his wife, Muriel, had cared for him for years, and for that he was in her debt. But more than obligation, he *wanted* to care for her because it was an honor to care for the wonderful person that she had been and still was.

Messiah has come. He announced on J-Day that He would bring signs of healing to the world—and He did. But miraculous healings are just a hint of the total, complete healing yet to come when Christ returns to remake heaven and earth. In the meantime, we deal with injuries that may leave a soldier without a leg, with chronic illnesses that have no cure, and with common feebleness that accompanies the aging body.

But grace is stronger than it all.

In 2 Corinthians 12, the apostle Paul reveals something very personal. Besides continual threat to his personal safety, he suffered some kind of physical malady that he called a "thorn in the flesh." He doesn't say exactly what it was, but it was likely a physical problem. Because it was chronic, it was frustrating. He called it a "messenger of Satan" because God is not the source of pain. He prayed earnestly to be healed, and then he submitted to this higher reality: God's grace was sufficient for the day.

God's power is often seen more fully in weakness than in strength.

Make It Real: Pray today for someone you know who deals with chronic illness. Pray for that person to find God's grace for today, and if there is a loving act you can offer to demonstrate His grace, do it.

WEEK 5

GROUP DISCUSSION QUESTIONS

1. Have you ever wrestled with whether or not God still does miracles? Or whether or not He heals us physically as well as spiritually? Or if it is okay to pray for physical healing, or only to pray a confession of sins? What were the circumstances that led to these questions?

2. What answers have you found for those questions—if any?

3. Come up with some examples of the following kinds of healing: physical, emotional, spiritual and relational healing (both with God and others).

4. Read out loud the key passage from Day 32, James 5:14-15. What jumps out at you from those verses?

5. If what James says about "the prayer offered in faith will make the sick person well" is generally true (that is, most of the time we heal from our illnesses and injuries), what are some examples in your life of physical healing? Have you or someone you know experienced healing that is of a more extraordinary nature?

6. How do you feel about having other people pray for you when you need healing?

7. Can you think of someone who was "raised up" (as James 5 says), even though they were not physically healed? Is it easy or difficult for you to think of death as a kind of final healing?

8. In what ways do you stand in need of Jubilee healing at this time in your life?

WEEK 6

JUSTICE

Standing for What Is Right and Being an Advocate for the Downtrodden

I love stories about law and order. Mysterious crimes solved. Criminals tracked down by dedicated and skilled investigators. Courtroom dramas where the truth is meticulously laid out. National revolutions that overthrow ruthless tyrants.

I wish that justice happened more often and more consistently. God's call to His people includes being agents of justice. But what does that mean?

Justice is not the business only of police and courts; justice is God's great movement to put in order what has become disordered in a chaotic world. Atrocious crimes such as genocide, child abuse and torture are injustice written in capital letters, but in everyday life we face the train wreck that is humanity: confusion, disarray and mayhem that cry out for order to come again. There are days when we long for healing, redemption, freedom and Sabbath, and sometimes the way we get there is when God leads us to a place of more order. That order is *justice*.

In his Gospel, Matthew says that Jesus "leads justice to victory" (12:20). But let's be honest: That promise is a challenge for anyone's faith at one time or another—that one day justice will prevail completely, that it is never too late for justice. Is it ever too late for justice in Israel or Iraq or Albuquerque or Milwaukee? Is it ever too late for justice in your family?

The Right Ordering of the World

The dictionary defines justice as the quality of being fair and reasonable. That's accurate, but incomplete. Being fair and reasonable is good—if we could double the number of people in the world who are fair and reasonable, that would be revolutionary.

But the biblical idea of justice goes much deeper. As we all know and the Scriptures analyze with precision, the human race is not just in its present state. In the Hebrew Old Testament and the Greek New Testament, justice is directly related to the character of God and the character He intended our world to have. The biblical meaning of justice is *the right ordering of the world according to God's character and intentions*—which are always good.

In Leviticus 19 and Ezekiel 45, we read God's commands for "just weights and measurements." Cheating merchants sometimes used bogus weights to cheat their customers, offering them lesser goods than what the customers thought they were paying for. The scales of justice are only as good as the weights and measurements we use. The famous statue called "Justice" is a blindfolded woman holding a set of scales, symbolizing the hope that someone out there is measuring our problems and coming up with solutions, blind to personal preference and bias.

But this measuring goes far beyond the legal system: The right ordering of the world according to God's character and intentions can apply to the whole pattern of our lives—not just when criminal prosecution for theft or murder is required, but when we realize we have hatred or covetousness in our hearts and we ask God to bring order. Major chaos (such as murder) is always rooted in a lesser chaos (such as rage) birthed in the hidden places of the heart.

Justice is not just about crime and punishment. It is God's movement to bring order to a disordered world. Assisting millions of AIDS orphans is justice because it is unjust that their parent's actions put their families in mortal danger. Missions of mercy to the impoverished at home or around the world are justice because the right ordering of the world according to God's intentions includes the common sense distribution of food and shelter. In the modern world we cannot prevent drought, but famine is almost always preventable. The major reason people still starve today is that other human beings stand unjustly between them and the food they need.

Prisons can be places for justice. Charles Colson was convicted after the Watergate scandal and put in prison. In the decades since, through Prison Fellowship International, Colson has been an advocate of justice, trying to get people to see the criminal justice system as a way to reform people's lives rather than only as punishment. Colson knows, as do thousands of people involved in prison ministry, that when you visit someone in prison, it is as if you are visiting Jesus (see Matthew 25:36).

It's never too late for justice.

There is a wide-open opportunity here for all of us who look for a deeper sense of *real* purpose in life. If we can help, to whatever degree, to bring "right ordering" to someone else's life, we have signed on to God's mission of justice. But we will only do so if we are motivated not by a self-centered interest in getting justice for ourselves (which can lead to vigilantism) or by the impulse to satisfy the visceral drive toward revenge, but when we are motivated instead by compassion for anyone and everyone suffering because of the world's disorder.

Justice, Jesus and Jubilee

All of us who long for real justice in our lives and in our world can take our cues from that moment in history—the life and ministry of Jesus—when justice was proclaimed more loudly than ever before. This proclamation happened just as Jesus was subject to the plotting of enemies who thought they were putting things right, but instead were about to commit the greatest injustice the world has ever seen.

> But the Pharisees went out and plotted how they might kill Jesus. Aware of this, Jesus withdrew from that place. Many followed him, and he healed all their sick, warning them not to tell who he was. This was to fulfill what was spoken through the prophet Isaiah: "Here is my servant whom I have chosen, the one I love, in whom I delight; I will put my Spirit on him, and *he will proclaim justice* to the nations. He will not quarrel or cry out; no one will hear his voice in the streets. A bruised reed he will not break, and a smoldering wick he will not snuff out, *till he leads justice to victory*. In his name the nations will put their hope" (Matthew 12:14-21, emphasis added).

Some of the most important passages in the Gospels are where we see Jesus having a pivotal interaction and then an Old Testament prophetic passage is quoted (as Isaiah is here). The Gospel writers do this to explain how Jesus' life was the unfolding of a cosmic plan, put into place long before He ever showed up. Fulfillment of prophecy is meant to bolster our confidence so that we can know, for instance, that the claim that Jesus will "lead justice to victory" is not mere words, but the driving intent of God, something He spoke about across the ages.

In the first part of Matthew 12, we read about bitter conflicts between Jesus and the Pharisees and other so-called "religious experts" on matters of observing the Sabbath. Jesus and His disciples hand-picked some grain in the field to chew on, and the Pharisees called it "working on the Sabbath." More astonishing than that, Jesus healed a man with a shriveled hand, and they castigated Him for "working" a miraculous healing on the Sabbath. Now think about that; it's astonishing, really. They took a supernatural act of God—which stupefied and amazed and bolstered hope in the people—and let Jesus know that He really shouldn't be doing that on the Sabbath. It broke the rules, after all.

And so they plotted how they might kill Jesus.

How can human beings become so confused that they take a spectacular thing God has done and call it an evil thing, and then plot how to stand against it, even if it means murder? And how can they then think that the "righteous" thing they are doing is backed by God?

Nothing much has changed. As I write this, my 19-year-old daughter is sound asleep in bed, but a few days ago she flew back from Europe on a day when a plot was uncovered to blow up 9 or 10 transatlantic flights from Europe to the U.S. I recoil at evil that close. In their twisted way, these plotting men believed that they were going to carry out a God-honoring act. How do you begin to describe this mutation of human nature? It's morally upside down and spiritually rotten. It is a perversion of justice. And it's the reason we need God to roll across the human race with justice.

Living Where Things Are Not as They Should Be

We are living in a world where things are not what they should be (that's putting it mildly). In our world, things are turned inside out and upside down. Human beings forget what order even looks like. Some lose sight of what a rightly ordered family looks like; others can't remember a time when the nation in which they live had courts that worked or any kind of fairness in their economy.

We are living in times when we have to long for justice like never before. I heard some news analysts talking recently about the global struggle with terrorism and the conflicts in southern Lebanon, Afghanistan and Iraq. One person said that we aren't going to be declaring victory in the war on terrorism for a very long time. Another said that we have just begun a 100-year war. Someone else has said that the world has to see itself as living with a cancer. Another pointed out that more time has passed since 9/11 than the entire duration of World War II.

How do you respond to statements like these? How do you not lose hope?

On a more personal level, there are the situations we face that seem intractable, that seem as if we will never see justice. The boss who consistently demands ethically questionable practices. The husband whose wife perpetually blames him for everything wrong in her life, including things he has absolutely nothing to do with. The wife whose husband belittles and demeans her to keep her in her place. The cop who pulls over an African-American because he is driving in a predominantly white neighborhood . . . where he happens to live. The graduate student whose thesis committee fails her because one committee member has a grudge against her advisor. The believing Christian who is passed over for promotion because an inner circle thinks his convictions make him an oddball.

The life of Jesus Christ will always be our reference point for understanding what is right in life, for where we and the world have gone terribly wrong, and for where there is hope. Because there really is hope. A lot of people have buckled under the unbearable burden of injustice. They have been wronged and then wronged again. They tried to set things right, but the whole situation became a confused mess.

Things aren't coming together, but getting more tangled. One wrong has led to another. There is no justice.

At least not yet.

The Chosen Servant of God Proclaims Justice

There is a section in the prophecy of Isaiah in which he talks about "the servant of God" who will come, a "suffering servant" who will rescue the human race, but also suffer at the hands of the human race. Matthew paraphrases Isaiah this way:

> Here is my servant whom I have chosen, the one I love, in whom I delight; I will put my Spirit on him, and he will proclaim justice to the nations. He will not quarrel or cry out; no one will hear his voice in the streets (12:18-19).

God's Spirit comes and then justice is proclaimed—not just to a few thousand people in Galilee, but to the nations. This is, in fact, what happened when Jesus went into the Jordan River where the Holy Spirit descended on Him like a dove, and then went into the dry chalky hills of Judea where He was tempted by Satan, and then went to a synagogue in Nazareth where He opened the scroll of Isaiah and read similar words: "The Spirit of the Lord is on me, because he has anointed me to preach good news to the poor. He has sent me to proclaim freedom for the prisoners and recovery of sight for the blind, to release the oppressed, to proclaim the year of the Lord's favor."

The Jubilee. And it is all about Jesus—the One who was sent, the chosen Servant and Son of God who came to proclaim justice to the nations. And when it seemed as if His voice wasn't even going to get outside a small circle of people, when the authorities plotted how to kill him, He did not "quarrel or cry out." No one "heard his voice in the streets."

There's an application for Christian witness here. Proclamation may include confrontation, but it must not be based on complaining. No one was ever converted by Christian complaining. To confront injustice is one thing; to grouse and gripe about what we don't like just comes off as whining.

In what sense did Jesus proclaim justice to the nations? After all, He did not travel between the nations of His day. He had no passport; He boarded no planes to distant lands. He didn't have an Internet newsletter. He traveled by foot from town to town, and His life was lived in a tract of land less than 100 miles top to bottom. Yet His proclamation of justice did in fact extend to the nations. And His justice is the only hope for the nations today.

Compassion and Justice

Jesus-justice defines the cause. Justice is the flip-side of a single coin on which "compassion" is written on the other side. In analyzing all the attributes of God described in Scripture, Scottish theologian P. T. Forsyth concluded that there are two that summarize them all: *holiness* and *love*. Want to describe who God is? Forsyth settled on this: God is holy-love. Justice and compassion. Righteousness and advocacy.

For too long, people who read the Bible simplistically have put a dividing line between God's justice and God's love. The logical outcome of this is that people feel as if they have to make a choice: Pick a religion of law or a religion of love. Focus on the Old Testament or focus on the New Testament (as if the Old focused only on justice, and Jesus focused only on love . . . not true at all!).

God's justice and God's love are never separated, any more than God's own character can be bifurcated. God brings judgment *because* He loves. God reaches out in compassion *because* He sees the unjust things we do to each other. He has to set things right because that is what a caring God would do. Here is the heart of God:

> He defends the cause of the fatherless and the widow, and loves the alien, giving him food and clothing (Deuteronomy 10:18).

> I was a father to the needy; I took up the case of the stranger. I broke the fangs of the wicked and snatched the victims from their teeth (Job 29:16-17).

> He upholds the cause of the oppressed and gives food to the hungry. The LORD sets prisoners free, the LORD gives sight to the blind, the LORD lifts up those who are bowed down, the LORD loves the righteous. The LORD watches over the alien and sustains the fatherless and the widow, but he frustrates the ways of the wicked (Psalm 146:7-9).

"A bruised reed he will not break, and a smoldering wick he will not snuff out, till he leads justice to victory" (Matthew 12:21).

And so I ask myself, *Who might I meet today who is a "bruised reed," and will I notice? Will I recognize, as Jesus did, that person who is so beaten down, so disheartened, that he or she is a "smoldering wick"?* I should not assume that I will see these people, because my selfish human nature wants me to look past them, wants not to notice them. In my fallen nature I want justice for myself. I need God's Spirit to raise me to the level where I have a burning passion for justice for others.

The world is crooked. People—all of us—are bent. We look for law and order in part because we know it is right, but also because we don't want criminals to break into our homes. But in the words and deeds of Jesus is a call to justice that breaks us out of our small worlds and sweeps us up into a great mission and purpose God is unfolding in the world. The Messiah has come to "lead justice to victory."

"Lead" is a very strong word. He pushes it forward. He thrusts it out. God will never give up on justice, and so God's people must never give up. In the Old Testament that meant standing up for the widows, the orphans, the aliens, the poor, the prisoners, the slaves and the sick. In the Year of Jubilee, the people were required to come back to this high calling. To hit the reset button and remember.

It is never too late for justice.

Hope for the Nations

The passage in Matthew about Jesus-justice says that "in his name, the nations will put their hope."

As I write this, the world is in tension, the nations of the world like guns locked and loaded, ready for someone to pull the trigger. Is there any real hope for the nations? It's hard to believe in such a world.

On the one hand, I could be very discouraged. When I learned that the plot to blow up airliners flying from Europe to the U.S. was hatched by British citizens—some of them second-generation Brits—I was stunned, as was much of the world. These were people who have grown up in a Western country that highly values human life, law and order, education, healthcare and stability. Yet even these citizens, who have benefited from these institutions, could be radicalized and turned into instruments of purposeless murder.

At the funeral of a Supreme Court Justice in 1845, Daniel Webster said, "Justice is the ligament which holds civilized beings and civilized nations together." This is important: It is not civilization that civilizes people. Living in a Western country does not automatically make you a "civilized" person. Where I live in the U.S., it is as plain as can be that every year our culture becomes coarser and coarser. This is because civilization does not just "rub off" on you; there are choices for or against justice to be made along the way. There are unjust barbarians who live in hidden corners of the world just as there are unjust barbarians who are quoted as authorities in the best newspapers in the world.

No wonder we need Jubilee. We need seasons in life to hit the reset button, to come back to the essential things, to remember why we are here, to remember why Christ came. We all need God to put in order what has become disordered in our lives.

I want to have the courage to keep asking myself who I know in my sphere of influence for whom I could be an advocate of justice. Whom do I know who needs food and clothing, who is fatherless or motherless? Whom do I know who is in prison or is blind or disabled or ill in some way? Whom do I know who is a widow or a single parent? If it is within my power to bring justice or to advocate for justice, I must do so. In this way, hope is brought to the nations.

Justice comes from the Just One. And there is hope in Him.

Practical Steps to Becoming a Jesus-Justice Advocate

Years ago, I ran across a sentence that I knew in my gut had to be the guiding star of my life. It just reached out and grabbed me: "What does the Lord require of you? To do justice, and to love mercy, and to walk humbly with your God" (Micah 6:8). The Lord *requires* me to *do* justice. And so I pray this prayer: "Let justice roll down like waters, and justice like an ever-flowing stream" (Amos 5:24) and I get to work!

But what do I have to do to "do justice"?

1. Open My Eyes to Injustice at the Personal Level

I need a conversion of my natural self that makes me selective about what I see, biased in how I interpret it, and selfish about doing anything to stop it. I need to give up my tendency to gloss over problems, to look the other way, to blame people always for their own problems. I need to notice the "bent reeds" around me. I need to try to understand the wife and mother whose powerful husband is raking her over the coals in divorce court. I need to get at least a rudimentary understanding of what it is like to not have a home to go to at night. I also need to open my eyes to any injustice I am responsible for or participated in. Is there anybody I am taking advantage of? Am I relating to anybody out of bias and preference?

2. Open My Eyes to Injustice in My Community

My days fill up quickly with things that need to be done, with people who need my help, with the stories in the news I prefer to read. I've always struggled with having much interest in the local news, I think because news from around the world is big and bold. One day it is a spectacularly good story, such as the scientists who landed robotic machines on Mars and drove them around taking pictures for more than a year. The next day it is a dramatic story of hundreds of people killed in a terrorist attack, or some new revelations about an emerging nuclear nation. These stories are written in bold type and (conveniently for me) often take place thousands of miles away from where I live. I don't have to deal with them personally.

But the stories about my community are closer. They may not be in my neighborhood, but they are in my city. The local news sometimes seems to wallow in drug-house murders, a city council member accused of corruption and the latest storm being tracked by Doppler radar, but there are many other stories in my community, and probably a lot more *good* stories than I will ever run across in the world news! Here is the challenge: In between my tiny personal world and the big wide world are the real world and the real stories of law and order, corruption and chaos in my community. I must keep my eyes open to this world.

3. Open My Eyes to Injustice Around the World

It is not good enough for me to bemoan the troubles of the nations, to shake my head and cluck my tongue when I hear about civil wars and corrupt governments. I need to understand how genocide can happen, and do what I can to prevent it.

4. Do Something About What My Open Eyes See

And I must not lose hope. God has not given up on the human race. God is at work. China is changing because of Christians doing community work in small towns, bringing order where there was none. Sub-Saharan Africa is changing because a hundred years of explosive growth in Christianity has brought order where there was little. Men I know who used to be absentee fathers, working and drinking themselves to death, are different today because they found the Lord of order.

I cannot straighten out the world today and never will. But any little thing I do today to straighten out something in my life and to help straighten out someone else's life is a small victory in God's campaign for order.

DAILY REFLECTIONS

Day 36

If one of your countrymen becomes poor among you and sells himself to you, do not make him work as a slave. He is to be treated as a hired worker or a temporary resident among you; he is to work for you until the Year of Jubilee. Then he and his children are to be released, and he will go back to his own clan and to the property of his forefathers. Because the Israelites are my servants, whom I brought out of Egypt, they must not be sold as slaves.

LEVITICUS 25:39-42

She made her way onto the city bus after a long day and plopped herself down in a seat halfway back. As the bus approached the intersection of Moulton and Montgomery streets, a white man got on and could not spot an open seat in the first 10 rows—the designated white section. The driver told some of the blacks sitting in the middle to move farther back and a group of them did . . . all except 42-year-old Rosa Parks.

Later accounts say that her refusal was due to the fact that she was tired; Parks herself maintained that it was because she was tired of the same old thing. The law at the time stipulated that the first 10 rows were reserved for whites, while blacks had to enter via the back door of the bus and were required to move or stand if a white person wanted them to move. This was the law. So the bus stayed at that intersection with Rosa still seated until the police arrived and arrested her.

She didn't know that day that the evening of December 1, 1955, would be a turning point in history. The incident prompted a boycott of the bus system in Montgomery, Alabama, for 13 full months. The law was challenged, and finally ended up in a landmark case before the Supreme Court of the United States. The Court's ruling in 1956 that bus segregation is unconstitutional was one of the early tremors that eventually led to the collapse of institutionalized racism in the U.S.

Justice often flows slowly and imperceptibly. But when it does, it changes everything.

Down through the history of the world, the norm has always been that people use other people. So when the Bible makes a point to go against that grain, we must notice how important justice is as an overarching theme for God's people. The Year of Jubilee required the Israelites to let their slaves go free (instead of serving for life) and to treat their slaves as if they were hired workers. These challenges for God's people to move toward justice demonstrate Scripture's trajectory of justice, aimed toward the coming of Jesus, who was definitely *not* the same old thing.

Everyone is susceptible to treating others unfairly or unjustly, either in action or attitude. The beginning of the end of injustice is when we say that we're tired of the same old thing. We can do better than this.

Make It Real: Watch the news or read a paper today and look for one story of injustice that is the same old thing. Pray that God would move you from indifference to passionate advocacy.

Day 37

But let justice roll on like a river, righteousness like a never-failing stream!

AMOS 5:24

It was a time of tremendous optimism. Eight centuries before Christ, people were flourishing in the Promised Land. The prophets Elisha and Jonah had prophesied a time of resurgence and strength.

But there was a quiet infection going on within God's people. While they had wealth, peace with their neighbors and places of worship marked by spiritual vitality (or so they thought), there was something wrong in their hearts. Things looked good on the outside, but they were rotting on the inside.

People had begun to indulge in luxury. They blinked at immorality. They let the command to live justly slide. The world had seen it before, but no one thought it would happen in the middle of Yahweh's territory.

God gave a man named Amos, a shepherd from the small town of Tekoa near Bethlehem, an abrupt and stunning message: "I hate, I despise your religious feasts; I cannot stand your assemblies . . . Away with the noise of your songs! I will not listen to the music of your harps" (Amos 5:21-23). *Why?* Even if the functions and methods of worship are right, no one can worship rightly and claim fidelity to God as long as everything in his or her life contradicts it. You can't be righteous without loving the right. You can't expect justice if you don't stand for it.

"Let justice roll on like a river . . ." It doesn't matter how much sacrificial service we pour out of our lives, how many songs we sing in worship, how many checks we put in the offering plate; if we use people to our advantage, if we are indifferent toward the malaise of the masses, if we manipulate the justice system to our own ends, then we are living a lie.

Justice is not confined to law books and the courts. It is a living thing, and it gives life as surely as the steady stream of fresh water makes the trees and the fields flourish. And justice does this, too—it solidifies our faith in the one Just God.

Make It Real: On a world map, randomly select a country (that isn't yours!). Spend time in prayer today for that country. Pray for its people to see political justice and for it to be a place of peace.

Day 38

Is not this the kind of fasting I have chosen: to loose the chains of injustice and untie the cords of the yoke, to set the oppressed free and break every yoke? Is it not to share your food with the hungry and to provide the poor wanderer with shelter—when you see the naked, to clothe him, and not to turn away from your own flesh and blood? Then your light will break forth like the dawn, and your healing will quickly appear; then your righteousness will go before you, and the glory of the LORD will be your rear guard.

ISAIAH 58:6-8

Comments from Bono, lead singer of U2 and Christian activist, at the National Prayer Breakfast in Washington, DC, on February 2, 2006:

> In 1997, a couple of eccentric, septuagenarian British Christians went and ruined my shtick—my reproachfulness.

They did it by describing the Millennium, the year 2000, as a Jubilee year, as an opportunity to cancel the chronic debts of the world's poorest people. They had the audacity to renew the Lord's call . . . What was this Year of Jubilee, this year of our Lords favor? I'd always read the Scriptures, even the obscure stuff. There it was in Leviticus: "If your brother becomes poor," the Scriptures say, "and cannot maintain himself . . . you shall maintain him" (25:35).

From charity to justice, the good news is yet to come. There is much more to do. There's a gigantic chasm between the scale of the emergency and the scale of the response. It's not about charity after all, is it? It's about justice. Let me repeat that: It's not about charity; it's about justice. And that's too bad. Because you're good at charity. Americans, like the Irish, are good at it. We like to give, and we give a lot, even those who can't afford it.

But justice is a higher standard. Africa makes a fool of our idea of justice; it makes a farce of our idea of equality. It mocks our pieties, it doubts our concern, it questions our commitment. Sixty-five hundred Africans are still dying every day of preventable, treatable disease, for lack of drugs we can buy at any drug store. This is not about charity, this is about Justice and Equality.

A number of years ago, I met a wise man who changed my life . . . And this wise man said: *Stop.* He said, "Stop asking God to bless what you're doing. Get involved in what God is doing—because it's already blessed." Well, God, as I said, is with the poor. That is what God is doing. And that is what He's calling us to do.

Make It Real: Become better informed today about a ministry in the world where the people live in impoverished situations. Reflect on how you can make a difference.

Day 39

Here is my servant whom I have chosen, the one I love, in whom I delight; I will put my Spirit on him, and he will proclaim justice to the nations. He will not quarrel or cry out; no one will hear his voice in the streets. A bruised reed he will not break, and a smoldering wick he will not snuff out, till he leads justice to victory. In his name the nations will put their hope.

MATTHEW 12:18-21

Forty-one-year-old Abdul Rahman stood before a judge in Kabul, Afghanistan, to answer for accusations that he had converted to Christianity. He did not deny the charge. He did not deny the Bible put before him as evidence. He had become a believer in Christ 16 years earlier while working with a group that was engaged in a medical mission.

The Afghan court was in a bind. The new constitution of their country allowed for at least limited freedom of religion, but according to cultural Islamic standards in Afghanistan, apostasy from Islam was punishable by death. A gathering of 500 clerics and students demonstrated at a mosque, demanding that Abdul either return to Islam or face death. A senior cleric declared that if the courts did not bring "justice," then he would incite people to "pull him to pieces."

In the end, the incident became an international spectacle. Presidents, prime ministers and the Pope made appeals for mercy. And maybe no one would have noticed this "bent reed" if not for Hussain Andaryas, an Afghan Christian living in the West who spoke up on Abdul's behalf, focusing widespread media attention on his case and putting the spotlight on the injustice.

Justice is something to be won. Human beings don't passively slide into justice. The terrible disorder of this world does not get straightened out unless people, acting in response to God's call for order, get into action and put things in order.

The world cannot have too many justice advocates. Someone had to speak up for Abdul Rahman because his personal plea for justice would not have changed anyone's mind. There is not a day that passes when we cannot advocate for justice. We need to tell other people and tell the authorities when we see an injustice—to do that for great causes in the world, and for the ordinary people we know. Each of us can echo the words of the prophet Amos: "Let justice roll down . . ."

Make It Real: Search the Internet today for the phrase "persecuted church." Read one or two real-life stories and reflect on these stories of courage under pressure. Pray for your brothers and sisters in Christ who live in parts of the world hostile to their faith.

Day 40

For I was hungry and you gave me something to eat, I was thirsty and you gave me something to drink, I was a stranger and you invited me in, I needed clothes and you clothed me, I was sick and you looked after me, I was in prison and you came to visit me . . . Truly I tell you, whatever you did for one of the least of these brothers and sisters of mine, you did for me.

MATTHEW 25:35-36,40

Gary Waddingham, rector of St. Luke's Episcopal Church in Billings, Montana, tells this story:

> Several years ago, when I was ministering in a small rural community, we had extra food left over from our Christmas basket. I happened to think of a poor family who lived at the edge of town. I packed up the food and drove to their house. I am never sure how one goes about "doing charity" while preserving the dignity of those who receive the charity. When the woman, surrounded by her several children, answered the door, I thought of a subtle way to offer the food to her. I asked, "Do you know anyone who could use some extra food?" "You bet," she said and got her coat, headed toward her car saying, "Follow me." She took me to people who were poorer than she, people who desperately needed food. Even though she herself needed food, I remember clearly that there was absolutely no hesitation on her part.[1]

Social justice is not an abstract principle; it's about *people.* Real people. Jesus couldn't have made it clearer: "Whatever you did for one of the least of these brothers and sisters of mine, you did for me" (Matthew 25:40). Notice that He calls the stranger, the naked, the ill, the prisoner and the poor "brothers and sisters." More remarkable yet, He says that to show grace to one of them is as if we blessed Jesus Himself. What could be a clearer sense of direction for any of us, a stronger sense of calling?

The possibilities are endless. We don't need to wait until we find just the right charitable organization whose operations are impeccable and cause is worthy. We can do something today. Any society has multitudes of disadvantaged people. Jesus said, "Whatever you did . . ."

Make It Real: Do one thing today for someone who is among "the least of these." Bring some clothing to a resale shop. Drop a check in the mail to an organization that assists the poor. Offer to help a single mom in your neighborhood or in your family. Write a letter to someone in prison. And if you conclude that there is a big gap between yourself and needy people, ask yourself why and think of a way to begin to close that gap.

Day 41

The Spirit of the Lord is on me, because he has anointed me to preach good news to the poor.

LUKE 4:18

Some issues are complicated or even ambiguous in Christian ethics. The issue of Christian response to the poor, however, is absolutely unambiguous. The Old Testament, the New Testament, and in particular, the teachings of Jesus sound a clarion call: God has compassion for the poor. God will judge those who oppress or take advantage of the poor, and He calls His people to alleviate their suffering. Let the words of Scripture itself ring out:

> Do not mistreat an alien or oppress him, for you were aliens in Egypt. Do not take advantage of a widow or an orphan. If you do and they cry out to me, I will certainly hear their cry (Exodus 22:21-27).

> He who oppresses the poor shows contempt for their Maker, but whoever is kind to the needy honors God (Proverbs 14:31).

> Woe to those who make unjust laws, to those who issue oppressive decrees, to deprive the poor of their rights and withhold justice from the oppressed of my people (Isaiah 10:1-3).

> He who is kind to the poor lends to the LORD, and he will reward him for what he has done (Proverbs 19:17).

> Now this was the sin of your sister Sodom: She and her daughters were arrogant, overfed and unconcerned; they did not help the poor and needy (Ezekiel 16:49).

> For I know how many are your offenses and how great your sins. You oppress the righteous and take bribes and you deprive the poor of justice in the courts (Amos 5:12).

> If anyone has material possessions and sees his brother in need but has no pity on him, how can the love of God be in him? (1 John 3:17).

The "good news" that Jesus proclaimed to the poor is not just that He loves them, but that He has called vast armies of His people to their aid. Will we obey God or not?

Make It Real: Find out today what avenues your church or community of faith is committed to in the cause of compassion for the poor. Talk with a leader to see how you can get involved.

Day 42

You give a tenth of your spices—mint, dill and cummin.
But you have neglected the more important matters of the law—
justice, mercy and faithfulness.
MATTHEW 23:23

In the early 1990s, police in South Dakota apprehended a man for committing a string of robberies. In his wallet they found a curious written statement, a kind of robber's code of ethics: (1) I will not kill anyone unless I have to; (2) I will take cash and food stamps—no checks; (3) I will rob only at night; (4) I will not wear a mask; (5) I will not rob mini-marts or 7-Eleven stores; (6) If I get chased by cops on foot, I will get away. If chased by vehicle, I will not put the lives of innocent civilians on the line; (7) I will rob only seven months out of the year; (8) I will enjoy robbing from the rich to give to the poor.

This modern-day Robin Hood had his own standard of justice. The South Dakota court, however, did not judge him according to his standard. He was tried and convicted by a higher law, a law derived from the Ten Commandments.

It is not enough for us to have any old standard of justice for our lives. Real justice comes from above, drawn from the inexorable laws of God that define and protect the dignity of life. If the standard of justice is arbitrary to anybody, it is useless for everybody.

We are fascinated by stories about law and order—in film, television, plays and novels. We always want to see the bad guys get caught. But justice, from a biblical point of view, is not just about punishing the criminal; it is about pursuing what is right in the first place.

Jesus confronted the most religious people of His day, the Pharisees, about their petty standards: "You give a tenth of your spices—mint, dill and cumin. But you have neglected the more important matters of the law—justice, mercy and faithfulness." The Pharisees were living according to their own standards of righteousness, but justice means celebrating what is right—and living it.

Make It Real: Read the Ten Commandments (Exodus 20:1-17) today. Identify one of them that needs further application in your life at this time. Remember that because you are redeemed and freed, transformation can take place.

Note

1. "Needy Woman Gives to Others" from PreachingToday.com. http://www.preachingtoday.com/illustrations/weekly/04-12-13/15668.html (accessed May 2008).

WEEK 6

GROUP DISCUSSION QUESTIONS

1. Identify some stories of justice in our culture today from movies, books or news stories.

2. What is in the news today (from your community or the world) that is a matter of justice?

3. What is one great injustice in the world that stirs you up?

4. What is a great personal injustice you have witnessed in the life of someone you know?

5. What are some reasons we are passive instead of being God's mouthpieces for justice?

6. How does the biblical ideal of justice ("the right ordering of the world according to God's character and intentions") go way beyond the common idea of "the quality of being fair and reasonable"?

7. What are some practical ways we can speak up on matters of justice?

8. How can we make sure that our pleas for justice are just, and not merely our preferences and opinions?

WEEK 7

PROCLAMATION

Knowing What You Stand For and Letting Others Know It

Abraham Lincoln was destined to become one of the greatest champions of freedom and justice the world had ever known, but early in his presidency he was viewed as controversial and divisive. Some people even saw him as a gigantic loser. And when he took up a pen to sign the document called the Emancipation Proclamation, which said that "all persons held as slaves . . . are, and henceforward shall be free," Lincoln was asserting something to be true that had yet to be realized in fact. It was a controversial and (some said) divisive act, and many wondered at that stage in the Civil War if the president had what it took to win. But that is the power of proclamation: Many historians see Lincoln's freeing of the slaves as the turning point of the War. When a person of adequate power and authority proclaims something to be true, it is the beginning of real change.

But it may not happen quickly. In fact, on the day Lincoln put his signature on that document, nothing at all changed in the lives of men and women held as slaves. It took months and years for the effects to turn the tide of America's "original sin." But because President Abraham Lincoln proclaimed freedom for slaves, everything changed.

The J-Day Proclamation

At the beginning of this book, we looked at the explosive and world-changing proclamation that Jesus made at the start of His ministry when He went into the synagogue of His hometown. He proclaimed the fulfillment of a pivotal ancient prophecy.

Hundreds of years earlier, the prophet Isaiah bore the burden of delivering the oracles of God to His people. The words of Isaiah 61:1-2 flowed by God's Spirit through the reluctant prophet:

> The Spirit of the Sovereign LORD is on me, because the LORD has anointed me to preach good news to the poor. He has sent me to bind up the brokenhearted, to proclaim freedom for the captives and release from darkness for the prisoners, to proclaim the year of the LORD's favor and the day of vengeance of our God, to comfort all who mourn, and provide for those who grieve in Zion—to bestow on them a crown of beauty instead of ashes, the oil of gladness instead of mourning, and a garment of praise instead of a spirit of despair.

Like most prophetic oracles found in the Old Testament, the words had an immediate application. Among God's people in Isaiah's time were many who were poor, brokenhearted, held captive and in mourning. To those people, beloved by God, Isaiah announced his role: "The Spirit . . . is on me, because the LORD has anointed me to preach good news . . ." But even as Isaiah spoke these words from God's heart, he may have sensed that they belonged to Someone else, too. The words were bigger than him. The words echoed. Isaiah may have known that he was sounding a message that would one day be brought to completion by the Chosen One, God's own Messiah.

And so it was that seven centuries later, a 30-year-old man stood in the synagogue of His hometown of Nazareth—a gathering room He had likely been in many times, made of stone walls that made the speaker's voice echo. And every word He read from the scroll of Isaiah echoed far beyond that place.

God was bursting forth in a new way. Just weeks before, Jesus had been in the Jordan River with His cousin John the Baptist, who was immersing people ready to humble themselves and come to God for cleansing. Jesus didn't need cleansing, but He needed to set an example. As He was in the water, the voice of God the Father rang from heaven: "You are my Son, whom I love; with You I am well-pleased," as the Spirit descended on Him in bodily form like a dove (see Matthew 3:16-17). The voice of the Father, the descent of the Spirit and now the mission of the Son.

He announced His mission with the greatest proclamation the world has ever heard:

> "The Spirit of the Lord is on me, because he has anointed me to preach good news to the poor. He has sent me to proclaim freedom for the prisoners and recovery of sight for the blind, to release the oppressed, to proclaim the year of the Lord's favor." Then [Jesus] rolled up the scroll, gave it back to the attendant and sat down. The eyes of everyone in the synagogue were fastened on him, and he began by saying to them, "Today this scripture is

> fulfilled in your hearing." All spoke well of him and were amazed at the gracious words that came from his lips. "Isn't this Joseph's son?" they asked (Luke 4:18-22).

It was a proclamation of *freedom*. Joseph's son proclaimed "freedom for the prisoners." There were many people in Israel at that time who felt as if they were in bondage. There was a new "Pharaoh" in the world, but he lived in Rome and had a mighty empire that swallowed people whole. He was called Caesar.

It was a proclamation of *healing*. Joseph's son proclaimed "recovery of sight for the blind." *What could that mean?* They could only guess that day, but soon enough they heard the rumors as Joseph's son moved about Galilee doing miracles like no one had seen since the age of Elijah and Elisha.

It was a proclamation of *justice*. Joseph's son proclaimed "good news to the poor" and release for the oppressed. *What does He know that we don't?* He had no wealth. He wasn't, as far as anyone knew, part of the underground movement to overthrow the occupying Roman army. Or maybe He was secretly one of those terrorists—the Zealots—who lurked in the night to slit the throats of Roman soldiers! No, Joseph's son wouldn't be one of the Zealots.

It was a proclamation also of *redemption* and *forgiveness* and a new era, a new *Sabbath*, in which God's people were to stop what they normally do so that everything could be different.

Their eyes were fastened on Him, struck with admiration by His graciousness, but Jesus knew their fascination would not last long. And He was right. "No prophet is accepted in his hometown" (v. 24), He said, implying that they would reject His message, that Gentiles might be more inclined to believe what was about to unfold. At these words, a spirit of anger and hatred filled the place, and they drove Jesus out. Pushing, shoving, kicking. They pushed Him out, right to the edge of the town, right to the edge of the cliff on which Nazareth was situated, and their rage kept them pushing. Push out the insult. Push away the confrontation. Push off the proclamation. It was as if a dark spirit descended on men who otherwise greeted each other on the street with a friendly "*Shalom.*"

When someone makes a proclamation, when someone takes a stand, it can lead to life. Or it can lead to someone getting hurt. Have you ever had to take a stand for something when you knew it might be perceived as a bald-faced insult? Have you ever told a truth to someone—a word that would liberate them—but their ears were closed to it?

That's exactly what happened when Jesus proclaimed Himself as the fulfillment of Jubilee. Take a look for just a moment in the last book of the Bible, Revelation:

> On the Lord's Day I was in the Spirit, and I heard behind me a loud voice like a trumpet, which said: "Write on a scroll what you see and send it to the seven churches . . . I turned around to see the voice that was speaking to me. And when I turned I saw seven golden lampstands, and among the lampstands was someone "like a son of man" (1:10-13).

The apostle John goes on to describe the appearance of this "son of man," and then:

> When I saw him, I fell at his feet as though dead. Then he placed his right hand on me and said: "Do not be afraid. I am the First and the Last. I am the Living One; I was dead, and behold I am alive for ever and ever!" (vv. 17-18).

Jesus announced the fulfillment of Jubilee on J-Day in Nazareth's synagogue. He could proclaim it with such certainty because Jesus *is* the Jubilee.

Our Proclamation

Now here is something extraordinarily important: Jesus' proclamation has become the proclamation of His followers. Anyone who counts himself or herself a follower of Christ bears a most sober responsibility: to keep the proclamation going. Just as Abraham Lincoln proclaimed emancipation for U.S. slaves and then generations of people worked to make that freedom real, so it is with Christ and Christians.

What is our proclamation? It is the life of Christ, and the life of Christ in us.

There are two main words translated as "proclaim" or "proclamation" in the Greek New Testament: *kerygma* and *evangel*. *Kerygma* refers to the proclamation of Christ's life, His *coming* as the proclamation, as the clarion call, as the trumpet sound—Jubilee. *Evangel* refers to the proclamation of the *content* of His message, the Good News Jesus proclaimed that everything in life is different when you live in the kingdom of the Messiah.

Colossians 1:28 says, "We proclaim him, admonishing and teaching everyone with all wisdom, so that we may present everyone perfect in Christ." For the apostle Paul, the purpose of *kerygma* and *evangel* were clear and focused. Later in Colossians 4:3-4 he says, "And pray for us, too, that God may open a door for our message, so that we may proclaim the mystery of Christ, for which I am in chains. Pray that I may proclaim it clearly, as I should."

Paul didn't ask for the doors of his prison to be broken open so that he could become a free man; he knew that he was already free. He asked instead for a doorway to open for the message. He calls that message about Christ a *mystery*. The message is, in part, about the concrete details of Messiah's birth, life, teachings, cruel death, resurrection and ascension. But the mysterious message is much more than the historical details about the life of Jesus. The message is not merely biography; it is the proclamation of the mystery of Christ's life *in us*. Jesus' life is a mystery in the sense that it continues on—exceeding expectations, boggling minds, crippling pride and arrogance. The mystery of Christ's ongoing life overshadows invented religions, outlasts empires and surpasses nationalism. The mysterious, Jubilee life of Christ continues to bring redemption, freedom, forgiveness, healing and justice.

That's why one of Jesus' closest followers, the apostle John, wrote in his first epistle that Jesus is, to us, "the Word of life."

> That which was from the beginning, which we have heard, which we have seen with our eyes, which we have looked at and our hands have touched—this we proclaim concerning the Word of life. The life appeared; we have seen it and testify to it, and we proclaim to you

> the eternal life, which was with the Father and has appeared to us. We proclaim to you what we have seen and heard, so that you also may have fellowship with us. And our fellowship is with the Father and with his Son, Jesus Christ. We write this to make our joy complete (1 John 1:1-4).

Our proclamation about Jesus Christ—the Jubilee—is about a man whom John touched and heard and saw with his own eyes. It is about the ongoing life of Jesus Christ, mystery of all eternity—Jesus Christ, the author of life, who laid down His life in a saving action of pure love and now lives through all who claim Him as their Jubilee.

Now, this "mystery of Christ," the "Word of life," naturally leads to a proclamation about all of life. In Acts 20:27, we read that the apostle Paul told a group of church leaders that he had not failed to proclaim to them the "whole will" (or "whole counsel") of God. A lot of people talk about the necessity for us to proclaim the whole counsel of God, but most of the time they are referring to some aspect of the message they believe has been neglected. But we must not miss what the phrase means. Paul had spent two years with the believers in Ephesus—working, eating, living with them—teaching the whole counsel or whole will of God. His message, given to them in word, deed and relationship, was about every single aspect of life—God's will and counsel at work in every area.

Followers of Christ, like Paul, know that the message of Jesus' life addresses every issue we face every day: *How should I control the pace of my life? What should my priorities be? Where should*

I work? Whom should I marry? How can I guide my kid when he's in trouble? What should I spend my money on? Why can't I seem to save any money?

What Christ-followers get to proclaim, in other words, is that God has counsel for us—the very best counsel we could ever possibly receive—that touches on every aspect of life.

What Do You Stand For?

It boils down to this: *What do we stand for?* What do we hold with such conviction that we are willing to proclaim it to someone else? And what will we proclaim, specifically and concretely, because the world does not need a lot of Christ-followers who go around blabbering generalities and platitudes.

More than 20 years ago when I heard in our church's staff meeting about the new phenomenon of HIV/AIDS, I have to confess that it sounded like someone else's agenda. After all, why should victims of a disease passed on by promiscuity become a significant issue for the Church? That was what I thought before I learned about the millions of kids who have been orphaned because of AIDS. That was before I met a person suffering from the disease. Someone put it this way: If you saw a car crash on the side of the road that happened because of reckless driving, would you pass on by, not even bothering to call 911? (Because that person should have known better, right?) No. No decent person would do that.

And that was before I stopped to remember that the early Christians' proclamation surged ahead when they did things like taking care of people in the aftermath of a plague in Rome. The anti-Christian, pagan emperor Julian at the time wrote that the early Christians "not only feed their own poor, but ours also . . . while the pagan priests neglect the poor, the hated Galileans devote themselves to works of charity."[1] No wonder Christian witness in those days rolled mightily across the empire.

In order for our proclamation to make a real difference in the world around us, we must submit to the call of the Messiah and live completely in "the year of the Lord's favor." We must live a Jubilee life.

Then we need to deepen and broaden our understanding of the message of Christ. For 20 centuries, various Christians have tried to boil the gospel down to one thing . . . and have thereby reduced the Good News. Some have said that the Church exists to administer the sacraments. Others, that the Church is to transform barbarism into civilization, or to conduct acts of mercy to the poor, or to preach the Bible, or to preach the death and resurrection of Christ. And of course, the answer is that the Church exists for all these things. Proclaiming the whole counsel of God is not a small thing. The message does not touch on just one issue of life, but all of life. It is a proclamation that is loud as a trumpet. It takes your breath away.

Pointing People to God

Proclamation means pointing people to God with the right word at the right time. It's been called "evangelism"; it's been called "witnessing." Communicating well with words always has been and always will be central to Christian proclamation, though pointing people to God is not limited to words. But when are words appropriate, and what words should we use? Where do we get the courage to speak up, and how do we match our courage with wisdom?

Here is one practical suggestion for an effective verbal witness: Dialogue opens the door to touch people's hearts. There is nothing new about this, really. Dialogue was Socrates's preferred method of teaching; and in his epistle, James says that we should be "quick to listen, slow to speak." If you want to proclaim the message of Jesus to your sister or your father or your neighbor because you know they need to hear it, don't prepare a 15-minute monologue. The other person wants you to understand his or her questions and dilemmas.

Words are important, but we can also point people to God through deeds of forgiveness, redemption, healing and justice. Christ's life in us is powerfully demonstrated in our deeds when we offer forgiveness, point a way to spiritual freedom, heal someone who is hurting, or stand up for someone who is suffering injustice. Many people don't want to hear anything about the Christian gospel because they don't know that it is everything they have been looking for. Through our actions, we can proclaim to people that forgiveness can be found in Jesus, that they can find freedom from their guilt and obsessions in life, that they can be healed, that God can set injustice right. Maybe we can't change their circumstances, but we can help them look at their circumstances with a whole new eye.

When Abraham Lincoln signed the Emancipation Proclamation, not a single Confederate state changed its constitution to disallow slavery. Instead, hundreds of thousands of individual slaves believed Lincoln's words. They believed that they were free men and women because it was proclaimed that it was so. Two hundred thousand of these newly free men fled north and joined the Union Army, helping to win the war. And then the institution of slavery finally began to crumble.

For the first year and a half, the Civil War was fought over the secession of states. During that time, Lincoln did not sleep or eat well. There were more Union defeats than victories on the battlefield. Volunteers for the Union Army declined. Many people wondered why they were fighting a war at all, if the institution of slavery was to endure. What was the cause?

Lincoln knew that something bolder had to happen, something more righteous than pragmatic. In the fall of 1862, the president finally decided to do the right thing. He picked up that pen with a shaky hand and made his proclamation.

And in the end, he took a bullet for it.

When you take a stand for something—a matter of principle, an issue of truth or a call for justice—you may find that you tremble, both because of the greatness of the truth and because you know some people aren't going to like it. Yet proclamation is the boldest thing any of us can do in life—to know our convictions and take a stand on them.

We make a proclamation when we . . .

- Befriend people who don't have many friends
- "Just say no" to drugs
- Go on a mission team to Biloxi, or to Mississippi, or to Tijuana, Mexico
- Show that you can have a good time at a party without getting smashed

- Say, "I'm not going to that event because I know all kinds of junk will happen"
- Refuse to take part when a rigorous gossip session begins
- Confront a fellow-believer who is running down his church
- Play softball in a prison with the church team
- Organize a Bible discussion in the office over the lunch hour
- Treat the restaurant server like a person and leave him or her an extra tip
- Show an act of mercy to someone who has just lost a loved one
- Talk about who Jesus really was when a discussion comes up about a movie that misrepresents Him

Decide that in the weeks to come, you will take your stand on life-changing Jubilee principles such as redemption, freedom, forgiveness, healing, justice and Sabbath. Be grateful for all the wonderful things God has done for you, and in the lives of others you know. Be confident, because no one can question the integrity of your experience of Christ's life in you. Let others know! But keep in mind that you don't have to proclaim everything at once. Just point people toward God, one step at a time.

Note

1. Julian the Apostate quoted in Thomas E. Woods, Jr., *How the Catholic Church Built Western Civilization* (Washington, DC: Regnery Publishing, 2005).

Day 43

Then have the trumpet sounded everywhere on the tenth day of the seventh month; on the Day of Atonement sound the trumpet throughout the land. Consecrate the fiftieth year and proclaim liberty throughout the land to all its inhabitants.

LEVITICUS 25:9-10

The president was in his upstairs study with a few friends—no cabinet members, no officials, just people who were close to him—and his hand paused as he took up the pen to place his signature at the bottom of the five-page document. His hand was shaking so violently that he couldn't sign. He collected himself and put his name at the bottom of the biggest gamble of the century—what would become one of the most famous documents in U.S. history: the Emancipation Proclamation. Abraham Lincoln used the power of proclamation to declare something true, despite the reality that life in the country looked entirely different.

Nothing changed on that day. The North was locked in Civil War with the South. Human beings were bought and sold, used and abused by other human beings. But *everything* changed on that day, too. Because when a proclamation is founded on truth and justice, the very act of proclaiming serves as a catalyst for transformation.

Jubilee is a proclamation. God commanded in Leviticus 25 that every 50 years on the Day of Atonement, the trumpet should sound throughout the land, and a proclamation of liberty should go forth. It was not just a president or king or army making this proclamation; it was God Himself.

All of us have something we need to be liberated from. We all need to be forgiven and need to forgive. We all need rest and restoration. And it begins here: believing God's proclamation and then seeking the reality of it in our lives. Lincoln declared the people free before they were actually free—but because the proclamation had authority and justice behind it, the declaration became reality.

Make It Real: Proclamation is founded on truth. Read at least part of the Sermon on the Mount today (Matthew 5–7) and make a note of three great truths Jesus proclaimed that could become your proclamation in life.

Day 44

The heavens declare the glory of God; the skies proclaim the work of his hands. Day after day they pour forth speech; night after night they display knowledge. There is no speech or language where their voice is not heard. Their voice goes out into all the earth, their words to the ends of the world.

PSALM 19:1-3

If you spent a week in one of the small valley towns in the Black Forest of Germany, you'd find yourself continually pointed toward God. Without doing anything other than walking in the mountain trails amidst tall majestic pointed conifers and noticing the beautiful small churches and their steeples lining the valley, you would be reminded of God. What do a mountain peak, a tall evergreen and a church steeple all have in common? They all point upward. They point us toward God.

This is also what the life of a Spirit-filled believer does, and what a church that worships in Spirit and in truth does. They all point people to God. Or at least they should.

We make a mistake when we limit Christian witness to what we have called in the past "witnessing." Before a believer can speak "witnessing" words, he or she has to have a life that is a witness. People read other people like a book, and if the life of Christ is written there, they will see it. What could be better than to be one person in a line of other people who point a lost person in the direction of God?

That is one way of looking at proclamation. Whatever the truth of proclamation is—justice, redemption, freedom, forgiveness, Sabbath, healing—it ultimately is a proclamation of the existence of God and the intent of God. And that is what people really want to know: *Is there a God and is He really interested in and involved in my life?*

Make It Real: Think of someone today who needs to hear the proclamation that God exists and loves him or her. Write a note, send an email or tell that person face to face today.

Day 45

That which was from the beginning, which we have heard, which we have seen with our eyes, which we have looked at and our hands have touched—this we proclaim concerning the Word of life. The life appeared; we have seen it and testify to it, and we proclaim to you the eternal life, which was with the Father and has appeared to us. We proclaim to you what we have seen and heard, so that you also may have fellowship with us. And our fellowship is with the Father and with his Son, Jesus Christ.

1 JOHN 1:1-3

It wasn't all just words. At the beginning of His earthly ministry, Jesus stood in the synagogue in Nazareth and read from the Isaiah scroll (see Luke 4). He read about the One who would come and "preach good news to the poor," "proclaim freedom for the prisoners" and "proclaim the year of the Lord's favor," the fulfillment of the Year of Jubilee.

It wasn't all just words.

Many years later, one of Jesus' closest disciples, John, wrote a letter as an older man to followers of Jesus past and present: "That which was from the beginning, which we have heard, which we have seen with our eyes, which we have looked at and our hands have touched—this we proclaim concerning the Word of life" (1 John 1:1).

This we proclaim. First, Jesus made the proclamation, then His disciples made it, and so on to this day. By the time John wrote his epistle, there already were thousands of followers of Jesus in Israel, Asia, Europe and Africa. The proclamation was being fulfilled.

We live 20 centuries after these events. We know that faith in Christ has spread around the world to hundreds of millions of people. But each person needs to ask himself or herself, *Have I accepted the proclamation of Christ? Do I really believe that His coming has made everything different? And am I ready to proclaim Him wherever I can, however I can?*

Make It Real: If you have accepted Christ as your Savior, make your proclamation today, at work (let only positive words come out of your mouth), at the gym (invite someone to church) or at school (pray at lunchtime). By your words and actions, others will know that you are a follower of Jesus Christ. If you have not yet made your proclamation, reflect on what is keeping you from making it real in your life.

Day 46

God has chosen to make known . . . the glorious riches of this mystery, which is Christ in you, the hope of glory. We proclaim him, admonishing and teaching everyone with all wisdom, so that we may present everyone perfect in Christ. To this end I labor, struggling with all his energy, which so powerfully works in me.

COLOSSIANS 1:27-29

A woman remembers a bit of advice her father gave her many times when she was growing up: *Try to leave things better than you found them.* In college, she became a teacher for children with disabilities and knew that everything she did made a difference, made their lives better than she found them.

It goes against human nature to leave things better than you find them. The world is full of chaos. Things fall apart. Lives deteriorate. But the regenerative power of God is never far away; we can't lose hope that things can get better.

The apostle Paul wanted to make a difference. He was committed to leaving the world better than it was before he became a disciple of Jesus, and he believed proclamation was the key: "We proclaim [Christ], admonishing and teaching everyone with all wisdom, so that we may present everyone perfect in Christ."

That's an incredibly high ambition. How can anyone hope to make such a difference in another person's life that they can "present" that person as perfect? Of course, none of us can. If you're a parent, you would love to raise perfect kids (and they, of course, would like you to be perfect as well). We would all like to make the people in our lives get along all the time, mature into perfect character, praise us for making such a difference in their lives. But "perfect" as Paul uses the word here doesn't mean flawless–it means *complete*. Paul knew that the work he was doing to help people entrust their lives to Christ gave them every essential that they needed in life: the "glorious riches" of Christ and the "hope of glory" that comes through Christ's life in them.

We leave the world a better place when we know what is true, when we know what we stand for and when we proclaim those truths (the "riches of Christ") out of a pure love for others. It is not easy. Proclamation is steady "admonishing and teaching everyone with all wisdom," and sometimes it is "struggling." Thanks to God, the energy for the struggle comes from Him and "powerfully works" in us.

Make It Real: Make a commitment today to serve in your community within the next month. Mark the date on the calendar when you will paint at a homeless shelter, pick up debris along the roadside or in a park, or do fall yard work for an elderly person. Make a difference by leaving things better than before.

Day 47

Devote yourselves to prayer, being watchful and thankful.
And pray for us, too, that God may open a door for our message,
so that we may proclaim the mystery of Christ, for which I am in chains.
Pray that I may proclaim it clearly, as I should. Be wise in the way
you act toward outsiders; make the most of every opportunity.
Let your conversation be always full of grace, seasoned with salt,
so that you may know how to answer everyone.

COLOSSIANS 4:2-6

How do you think about prayer? Is it work? Is it pleasure? Drudgery? Joy? Struggle?

We have missed something if we have not seen the naturalness of prayer depicted in Scripture. We wonder what it could mean to be "always in prayer." Many strong believers down through the ages have answered the question this way: Devotion to prayer means a continual conversation with God throughout the day. It is an instinct to respond to life circumstances by saying something to God about it.

Proclamation, which means pointing people to God, happens when there is an open door. And there are always open doors around us, but we have to open our eyes to see them ("being watchful and thankful"). Prayer opens our eyes to open doors and gives us the courage to step through them.

The apostle Paul prayed that even though he was in prison, doors would open for the message of Christ to break out. Imagine that. He didn't ask for prayer that the door of the prison would open up (though he likely would have welcomed that). Instead, he wanted the door of a relationship or a passing contact to open up so that he could "proclaim [the mystery of Christ] freely."

From his prison, Paul has a message for all of us who freely have contact with people all day long: Fill your conversations with grace (words about the sweetness of God) and seasoned with salt (words that protect and preserve, words with flavor!). Know ahead of time how to answer everyone.

These sweet and flavorful words become natural to us as we spend more and more time in conversation with God. His language of proclamation becomes second nature as we talk with Him throughout our days and nights.

Make It Real: Take the time today to pray for people who have been closed to the truth and wisdom God provides. Pray that God opens the door of their hearts and directs them to a personal relationship with Him.

Day 48

For whenever you eat this bread and drink this cup,
you proclaim the Lord's death until he comes.

1 CORINTHIANS 11:26

Because mortar fire could rain down at any time, the Marines were told not to be in groups of more than five or six in any one place. So during the two-month siege of Khe Sanh, Vietnam, one Navy chaplain found himself scurrying from group to group every day to hold a brief service of communion. He had to get through 20 to 30 abbreviated services each day, so he cut the service down to seven minutes—just the minimal amount of words, a prayer, the bread and the cup. Many times over the weeks, a cry came from a wounded soldier asking not just for the medic, but for the chaplain as well.

Worship is not a spectator sport. It is not a consumer event. It is *proclamation*. To worship is to make a loud declaration to yourself, to God, to other worshipers, to your friends and family, and to the world, saying, "I know I am a child of God. I desperately need God every day, and I must worship."

Communion in particular is a proclamation. Paul said, "Whenever you eat this bread and drink this cup, you proclaim the Lord's death until he comes." That's why Jesus said to do it often. Eat the bread; drink the cup. Make a proclamation. Acknowledge the One who gives you life. Take a stand.

When a person takes communion (unless he or she does it in a completely thoughtless fashion), he or she is saying, "I eat breakfast, lunch and dinner to feed my body, but I realize that I am more than just a body. I am a living, eternal soul. And I need to be spiritually fed as well. I need the Lord Jesus Christ, who is the Bread sent from heaven. I accept the gift of forgiveness that is made possible by His shed blood. This is what I need. This is who I am. This is why I am spiritually alive. This I proclaim!"

The sound of this proclamation is so great that it can muffle the sounds of mortars falling all around.

Make It Real: Think about what your worship proclaims. Write down on paper what your worship time on Sunday says about your life. Does it reflect community with others? Obedience to God? An expression of love for God? Focus on these things as you enter into worship on Sunday.

Day 49

[Jesus] said to another man, "Follow me." But the man replied, "Lord, first let me go and bury my father." Jesus said to him, "Let the dead bury their own dead, but you go and proclaim the kingdom of God."

LUKE 9:59-60

They entered the white stucco building in the middle of Tel Aviv quietly. The small museum was not known to a lot of people, and they certainly didn't know that on this date, May 14, 1948, history would be made there. David Ben-Gurion entered from the quiet tree-lined street and, before the small gathering, banged his walnut gavel to call the meeting to order. There was only one item on the agenda. Ben-Gurion read a document that had been carefully prepared and conceived for more than a generation: The Declaration of Independence of the State of Israel. And with that proclamation, the first Jewish state in 19 centuries was born.

There was no fanfare. No public display of celebration. Egyptian fighter jets patrolled the skies above. Other countries were in a war stance, ready to pounce if such a move were attempted. Since the British had left months earlier, everybody knew that those seeking a Jewish homeland might attempt to assert nationhood, but no one thought a new Israel would stand a chance against the surrounding armies. The following day the armies of Egypt, Transjordan, Iraq, Syria and Lebanon invaded the territory . . . and no one knew what would happen.

It is one thing to proclaim a radical new way of life; it is quite another to make it a reality. When Jesus came declaring "the kingdom of God," He was using words familiar to everybody, but in a whole new way. When on J-Day He said that the "acceptable year of the Lord," the Year of Jubilee, had been fulfilled, He was saying that God was moving in to take over. God, whose rule could never be challenged, was now making His benevolent rule available in a whole new way. With the coming of Christ, God's rule had come. He would unveil His fatherly care and lordly judgment. Jesus said to many people, "Follow Me." And then He challenged them to proclaim the same thing He was proclaiming: a new kingdom had come.

What do you stand for in life? There is nothing better than to stand for this: God rules over all, so we will live like He does.

Make It Real: Think about ways you know God is all-powerful. Then prayerfully consider someone who you know feels powerless. How can you let him or her know that Christ is King? Find a way to proclaim to that person that he or she has access to His endless power.

WEEK 7

GROUP DISCUSSION QUESTIONS

1. How does the remarkable story of Abraham Lincoln and the Emancipation Proclamation hit you personally?

2. Why does it take courage to proclaim?

3. Does it come easy for you to speak up about God, or is it difficult? Why?

4. What good examples have you seen of someone proclaiming the truth of God to someone else, and what bad examples?

5. What Jubilee truth could be the main theme of your proclamation in this time of life: Redemption? Freedom? Forgiveness? Sabbath? Healing? Justice?

6. Who is one person you know who needs to be pointed toward God at this time in his or her life? How can you be a mountain peak, a tall tree or a church steeple for that person?

7. Is there anything you have proclaimed in the past that you now regret because you were mistaken? Is there something you should do to correct what you told someone else?

8. What has Jesus—the Lord of Jubilee—proclaimed to your mind and heart during this Jubilee experience?

LAST DAY, NEW START

Day 50

For my Father's will is that everyone who looks to the Son and believes in him shall have eternal life, and I will raise him up at the last day.

JOHN 6:40

This is the last day of a 50-day spiritual journey, but a new start for living on a higher plane. In this short span of pages, we've opened up seven life-changing Jubilee truths: Sabbath, redemption, freedom, forgiveness, healing, justice and proclamation. They are not abstract truths, but great sweeping movements of God that go back to the earliest history of faith in the Old Testament.

We have been contemplating seven life-changing words. But they are not just words, not just concepts. They are life itself. The point of the Year of Jubilee in the Old Testament was for God's people to take a pause from their normal patterns of living and come back to the essential building blocks of a healthy, God-filled life:

1. *Sabbath*: rehearsing that God and God alone is in control
2. *Redemption*: being freed by God's great acts of deliverance
3. *Freedom*: cherishing the liberty that God brings to every area of life

4. *Forgiveness*: accepting the mercy of God and letting go of those you've held in debt
5. *Healing*: letting God restore your spirit, your body and your relationships
6. *Justice*: standing for what is right and being an advocate for the downtrodden
7. *Proclamation*: knowing what you stand for and letting others know it

And then Jesus came. He arrested the attention of the human race like a great trumpet sounding through all nations and across the ages. But this trumpet call of Jubilee is also the call of Christ to each of us personally. It is not to "the world" in some generic sense. It comes to me and it comes to you. In the synagogue in Nazareth, He read about "the acceptable year of the Lord" and announced that it was all being fulfilled. Because He came, everything is different.

Fifty days come and go in the blink of an eye. Will you choose to live in the Jubilee from now on?

Make It Real: Commit today to using the next 10 months as a season to probe the themes of Jubilee more deeply, and to make them real in your life. List three ways you intend to do that.

ABOUT THE AUTHOR

Mel Lawrenz has authored or co-authored numerous books, including *Patterns: Ways to Develop a God-Filled Life* and *I Want to Believe*. He has been a pastor at Elmbrook Church in Brookfield, Wisconsin, for the past 27 years, succeeding Stuart Briscoe as senior pastor in 2000.

Mel was born in Chicago in 1955 and grew up in Green Bay and Ellison Bay, Wisconsin. He earned his B.A. in creative writing at Carroll College, his M.Div. at Trinity Evangelical Divinity School, and a Ph.D. in historical theology at Marquette University. During the past 20 years, Mel has also taught as an adjunct faculty member at the University of Wisconsin in Milwaukee, Wisconsin, and at Trinity Evangelical Divinity School.

Mel hosts a weekly radio interview program called *Faith Conversations* and maintains an innovative and interactive website at www.cometobrook.org, which features streaming interviews, articles, resources, and more.

Mel married his high-school girlfriend, Ingrid, in 1975, and they have two college-aged children. Mel's personal interests include almost anything that will get him outdoors, particularly if it is near a body of water.

For free materials to supplement your Jubilee experience, visit
www.elmbrookjubilee.org.

To find out more about Mel and his books and writing, visit
www.wordway.org.

For messages, interviews and other resources from Mel and Elmbrook Church, visit
www.cometothebrook.org.